The Life of the Party

How to Throw the Best Party You Ever Went to

*Over 365 Ideas to Give Your Party
Flair, Meaning and Vitality*

K Callan

Dedication

This book is dedicated to Jamie, Kelly, and Kristi who would not be content with normal parties.

Acknowlegements

As usual, this book is a collaboration. My designer, Tom Devine, taught me so many things and made this book look terrific. I am very grateful. David Nolte finally made everything work. Donna Cellar always inspires me. Shirley Dion, Judy Rothman, Cathy Roberts, Kelly Callan, Don Williams, Kristi Callan, Wendy Crisp, Sandra Watt, Laura Zucker, Jimmie Rae Weeks, The Los Angeles Library and The Sherman Oaks Library all gave their energies to some portions of this book. I am very appreciative.

Other Books by K Callan:
An Actor's Workbook
The NY Agent Book
The LA Agent Book
How to Sell Yourself As An Actor

Library of Congress Catalog Card Number: 91-065951
ISBN 0-9617336-6-7

Book design by Devine Design, Burbank, California
Illustrations by Joe Crabtree

Contents

Forward

A party at K's is always a joyful event, whether it's a 12-person brunch on the patio, a 6-to-8 P.M. New Year's Eve, or once, an all-girl slumber party. (As usual, I fell asleep, but I remember taking photos of the other girls in their new bikinis. K looks great in a bikini.)

Over the past six years, I've been to numerous of her shindigs, and each holds a special place in my memory. I've learned games I'd never played before (or since), enjoyed food any hostess would be button-popping proud of, and met colorful and interesting, and daring, people. K shows more imagination and courage in getting her guests to do goofy things — and love it — than any other host I know. There's always a lot of laughter at her gatherings.

So it's high time she decided to let us in on the secrets of her success. And now here they are: ways to prepare the house, creative invitations, recipes, games, all the details that make a party a smashing event. With this delightful book as a guide, even a novice can become "The Host or Hostess with the Mostest."

There's something here for everyone: Oscar Parties, Father's Day, Chinese New Year, Hootenannies. Personally, I'm planning to have a Foot Painting Party as soon as possible, then a Summer Solstice Party, then a Stitch 'N' Bitch, then a — but wait — I didn't mention the one special ingredient that sets parties at her house apart: the hostess' bubbling enthusiasm, her warmth, her goodwill and fun-loving nature, all of which imbue the proceedings with an unmistakable charm. K's book presents all the tools and writes about them with such verve that even reluctant hosts will itch to start painting feet and dying their hairs grey for 30th birthday celebrations.

If I'm gushing, it's only because I want to make darned sure I'm invited to K's next party.

Rue McClanahan

Introduction

*party (par/te), a social gathering for conversation, refreshments, entertainment, etc.,
2. a group gathered for some special purpose or task: a search party, etc.*

According to the dictionary definition, breakfast at my house is a party. Actually, according to the first meaning it's always a party at my house. We are always talking and eating and we entertain each other pretty well, too. But, for me and for the purposes of this book, I'm going to combine the first and second definitions and add the word *activity*.

Party: a social gathering for some special purpose or activity accompanied by conversation, refreshments and entertainment.

The element most often missing is some special purpose.

There is nothing worse than being invited to someone's house where there are rafts of people you've never seen before and the special purpose consists mainly of eating. And I'm not the only one who gets anxious. Studies show that up to 75% of people at social gatherings are uncomfortable.

Don't get me wrong, I *love* to eat. It's just that, under stress and/or boredom, I can be counted on to eat way too much and spend the entire evening staring at my plate (or glass) unless I make the superhuman commitment to talk to at least three people I've never seen before.

This may or may not turn out well.

But, invite me to a party where there is Square Dancing or "Trivial Pursuit" (which I am terrible at) or any other *activity* and I can manage not only to have a terrific time but even also to make a few friends in the process.

So, this book is a collection of excuses for parties and simple fun, sometimes dumb activities that can turn the most diverse group of guests into instant best friends, at least for the evening.

I am really partial to "dumb." There is nothing that is so much fun to me as having a real license to get together with people and act like a group of first graders. Let's face it, adulthood has taken a lot of zing out of life.

But you, with this book, will change that.

K Callan
October 15, 1991
Los Angeles, California

Party Process

1   Party Process

Did you ever go to a party where you painted with your feet?

Learned to tap dance?

Told lies and won a prize for it?

You can not only *go* to a party like this, you can give one.

What It Takes

A few years ago, on vacation, I was sightseeing with a friend. As we drove past a 7-11, I said,

"The next time we pass a 7-11, I'd like to have a Dr. Pepper."
Before the words were out of my mouth, he had made a U-turn, purchased an ice-cold DP and I was savoring it.
"Gee, this is great," I said. "Once I get started driving, I have a terrible time stopping my forward motion. I'm really impressed that you are able to do that."
"I have a hard time stopping, too," my companion explained, "
but I make the effort."

What a revelation! All those people who make life look easy may just be making more of an effort. The possibilities astound me.
So it is with successful party giving. Somewhere, someplace, someone is making the effort.
When you go to a party and have a splendid time, it's not because the air is better there or their home is naturally inviting. Someone actually cuts all those flowers and spends time putting them in all those cute little vases all over the house. Their garden doesn't grow magically. Even if they have a gardener, they also have foresight and take the time to be sure the gardener doesn't simply "mow 'n' go."

If the food is scrumptious, if the music is just loud enough, if you want to make all the guests your new best friends and you don't ever want to go home, then your host has gone to great effort. It doesn't matter how easy-going she is able to appear.

Remember, all the great artists in the world make it look easy and so can you — if you have ideas, organize yourself, and are willing to *make the effort.*

This book is going to give you hundreds of ideas *and* it's going to stimulate the idea part of your brain so those hundreds will become thousands. It will also teach you how to organize and prioritize your efforts depending on your time constraints.

Some parties require more effort than others. For example, my daughters and I were feeling a bit like orphans a few Thanksgivings ago, because there were only going to be the three of us and one guest for dinner. To give the day some "pizzazz," I asked everyone to wear something that would make them feel like one of the original Thanksgiving participants. Nothing big, just something that could be added to their clothes a few minutes before the meal.

So we cooked and played in the kitchen and five minutes before we sat down to eat, we dashed off to put on our costumes. One daughter combined a scarf and a feather to represent an Indian. Another found construction paper and fashioned a pilgrim hat. Our guest became a trapper by wearing a furry bedroom slipper as a hat. I used red crepe paper to make a ruff and comb, and (gobble, gobble, gobble) I was the second turkey at our table. There was a lot of fun and silliness that Thanksgiving. It was no longer a small family gathering: with a little effort, it was a party.

My friends, Carl Sautter and Paul Waigner, produce a fabulous ***Annual Pumpkin Carving Party.*** Guests are given pumpkins and happily spend the evening acting like kindergartners creating entries that look variously like "The Phantom of The Opera" logo and Buelah Witch. At the end of the evening, the pumpkins are judged and prizes are awarded. Competitive comments about "next year" are traded by the guests — the contest has become a tradition. And of course, there is wonderful food, music, and decorations. A lot of effort and a spectacular result.

It's important to keep one's perspective. Party books, by and large, have become adventures in pretty table settings and lovely food. *Form* has taken precedence over *content.* The reader says, "Look at this beautiful dish. I want to cook it. Who can I invite to eat it?"

Or worse, "Look at this beautiful food. I can't cook like that. I can't have a party." Prospective partygivers end up *not* giving parties because the living room needs painting, the dishes don't match, or they don't have enough chairs. Table settings have taken precedence over the food and the *look* of the food has taken precedence over the *taste of the food.*

Dinner for two becomes a party when ideas and effort make it special. Candle-light, flowers, stemmed glasses, music, add up to romantic thoughts. If that same couple colored Easter eggs, wore Easter Bonnets or rabbit ears and ate carrots, it would definitely be a different party.

What this book calls "the event" doesn't just mean recognizing the usual holidays like Birthday or Thanksgiving. What it does mean is the slant or twist that is going to make this Thanksgiving different from everyone else's Thanksgiving while retaining the traditional parts that answer our need for the familiar: adding that part of the celebration requiring the participation of the guests.

It's not enough for the guests to merely arrive and eat. Put those folks to work. Give them something to do. Make them feel useful and needed. Allow them to be entertaining and clever. They may groan at the outset, but they'll not only have a wonderful time, they will talk about the party for weeks.

For a sparkling party it's not the chairs and plates, it's effort, organization, food, people, an event and ideas. Then, of course, it's what you do with all that.

Party Generalities

If your party coincides with a known holiday (Easter, Christmas, St. Patrick's Day), you will probably want to look to that holiday's traditions for inspiration about activities. Fun things to do include not only the traditional dyeing of eggs, but might also include Bonnet Making or your own original version of the May Pole. Did you know that the origin of Easter is in ancient Pagan Fertility Rites? Gee, that certainly conjures up some original party game ideas to me!

Christmas, St. Patrick's Day, Halloween and other traditional holidays are covered in the TRADITIONAL HOLIDAYS chapter with ideas for original twists on those days plus old favorites.

The real challenge to the imagination is for parties not on a Celebrity Day. For these days you can come up with your own ideas — or you can check my "CALLAN"-DAR. I've found or invented a holiday for every day of the year! There's National Tap Dance Day, National Crayola Day, National Pig Day (I made those up) as well as Elvis's Birthday, National Pickle Week and Moonlanding Day (I didn't make those up, of course.)

The time of the year can be an inspiration in itself. Just be aware of what's going on. Right after Christmas with all the attending rich food, friends might really appreciate a quiet "soup-making" party where all gather to cook together and experience new recipes.

If you're giving a party in the dead of winter, things can get very grey. Other than Valentine's Day, the calendar is pretty empty. People are thinking about things like property taxes and preparing their income tax. With this thought in mind, you might want to plan a very silly party that will encourage people to "get out of themselves" and look on the lightest possible side of things. Games like Pit and Rummy Royal (the rules are in the chapter entitled GAMES) involve lots of energetic interaction and undignified behavior. Pit is a store-bought game about the stock market, so if you wanted to have people over and play that game, you might call it *Wall Street Night* and decorate with ticker tape and phony stock certificates.

These parties have already been awarded special dates on the "CALLAN"DAR, but I promise not to sue if you improvise a new date to suit yourself.

The second part of the book is divided into these kinds of parties and more — we'll discover new ways of giving traditional parties like anniversaries, showers, and birthdays; how to give regularly scheduled parties (for cooking, crafts, charades); large parties and evenings for two; and annual events.

The GAMES section examines specific game ideas. You can either use my games as they are or use those ideas to spark your own. Once stimulated you'll be surprised how your own imagination will go crazy.

A friend came up with great ideas for a Pig Party. For the daring: go down to the Police Station and holler, "Pig!" For the sloppy, "eat at a trough," and for the menu, "Don't serve bacon!" I don't know how usable these ideas are but they are funny! The main point is that faced with a "CALLAN"DAR that tells you that April 15 is National Go Fly a Kite Day, it seems like a natural to gather your most game friends, head for the park and fly kites. Part of the fun can be making the kites (you furnish the materials) or buy kites and have each person assemble his own. Prizes can be given for the kite that stays in the air longest, flies highest, never makes it up, etc., etc. Follow it all by a picnic with the whole group sharing cooking chores around a campfire or hibachi.

Things to Consider

Time of the year

Different kinds of inspirations will occur to you in the Summer than in the Winter. You're not going to want to cook soup on the Fourth of July or have 3-legged races in December. A patio party that would be lots of fun in June would require a whole different set of rules in December...even if you live in California. And sometimes these very dichotomies will inspire a great Christmas Party on July 25th or an unusual Halloween Party on April Fool's Day.

How you feel

If you just want to "see" your friends, but don't feel like going to any trouble, it's time for a pot luck supper. If you feel like dressing up, you can give a New Year's Eve party...even in the middle of August. Just tell everyone you didn't get the year off to a good start and want another chance and that you can all dress up for the event.

Time

The party ingredient that "separates the women from the girls" is *time*. It takes a lot of time to produce an exhilarating party. Not only the time it takes for the actual preparation, but the thought and imagination accompanying it. Thinking time, planning time, inviting time, cleaning time, shopping time, chopping time, etc. It's not something I have in me to do every day. The time factor absolutely cannot be stressed enough in partygiving. It doesn't always have to take that much time, but one always needs to budget time carefully.

You only get hassled if you haven't allowed enough time for a particular preparation, whether it be for chopping onions, setting the table or taking 30 minutes of quick recovery time for yourself before your guests arrive.

So, be sure to pick the party that suits your time constraints. It's not necessary to be elaborate. I used to have monthly game nights with the same cast of people and everyone contributed a dish. After we all ended up bringing Waldorf Salad one evening, we added food coordinator to our list of tasks.

On game nights we'd gather, eat and play whatever. Many of those gatherings were memorable, others simply a great time. They certainly required little preparation from me other than my one dish. Womens' magazines suggest it is efficient to have back-to-back parties. That way you can prepare the house, use the same flowers and duplicate some of the same food, if you like. I've tried it. I had a dinner party on Saturday night and a Sunday brunch. I had a good time, but it certainly "partied" me out for a while.

Cost

Some events require more money than others. Make sure you take a realistic overview of what is required to do it well.

Space

Be sure to weigh the amount of room you have available. A square dance party (requiring multiples of 8) would not be successful in my living room whereas I have plenty of room for Pictionary.

Group personality

Are these folks all adventurous? Athletic? Cerebral? A word game will appeal to one group but others won't be able to sit still long enough to figure out the answers.

Will it work?

Fantasy vs. Reality. Some party ideas are like movie plots: they sound good on paper but just "lie there" when translated to the screen. A friend of mine planned a party for her boss who was renovating an old mansion. The party idea was a Demolition Party where the guests were encouraged to be as destructive as possible. There was a wall and large demolition tools. Each guest was blindfolded and led to the wall. The guests who did the most damage to the wall won a prize. That party brought out the worst in all the guests and turned into a really frightening experience.

Guest's time constraints

Anytime from November 1 to January 2 is busy for everyone. If you are planning on giving a party that requires a lot of time, thought, energy, and commitment from your guests (elaborate costume parties, for example), do everyone a favor and schedule it during a less busy time of the year.

Part of this consideration includes giving guests enough notice, but not too much. I personally don't want to accept an invitation for two months from now. Who *knows* what they will be doing that far in advance. I love expending the energy when the mood is in me. Then it's fun. When it's not, why force it? A party is supposed to be fun for the host too!

Recuperation

It's important to lie fallow after a creative experience. Just as fields need rest to replenish themselves after many bountiful seasons, we too need a respite after we've been prolific. Don't let yourself get burned out.

In brief, the time of year, how you feel, time constraints, cost, space, group persona, workability, guests' time constraints and your own recuperation time are all important things to think about before initiating party plans. If systems are still go, it's time to begin to deal with all the fun things: sticky situations, party behavior, food, organization, ideas and event.

The Fun Things

One of my favorite words is "synergy." It means the joint action of components that, when combined, produce a total effect greater than the sum of the individual elements.

Synergy is what makes the difference between a good party and a great party. It's the result of combining the right people who, when mixed together, spark a successful evening. The key is who to invite to the event you have selected.

For everyday entertaining I find I am most comfortable with groups of no more than 20 guests. There are parties, of course, requiring a large cast. Like most people, I have several groups of friends. One group is the Grown-up group. I mean, they *always* wear matching accessories and jewelry. I don't feel those people interact well with my "Puerae Eternae" group of friends (as radio psychologist Dr. Tony Grant says, "eternal boys and girls").

There are my liberal friends and then there are a few conservatives I've picked up here and there.

I have one or two friends I really love, but they never let anyone else talk when they're around. I always entertain them solo and don't subject my other friends to their monologues.

My guest list is determined by many things. First of all, is it a holiday or am I just in the mood for a party? And what holiday is it? If it's the Fourth of July and I'm cooking outside and playing stupid games, I'm not going to invite the jewelry group. They'd be more comfortable at a more serious party were we play Charades. I mean, it's not brain surgery, but at least they get to feel literate. If I'm just in the mood for a party, I think about who I want to see and plan the party around that cast.

Invitation

If you want to send an invitation, adapt the invitation to the party. It's fun to send and delightful to receive. A friend of mine gave her husband a birthday party. She contacted the newspaper of his hometown for a copy of the front page on the day he was born. She reduced that page, via xerox, and designed a darling invitation with that as a background. (For those who are sensitive about the year, it's easy to smudge or doctor the incriminating evidence.)

Lottery tickets, balloons, toilet paper, color xeroxed copies of dollar bills (or fives for Lincoln's birthday) are all ideas to spark your imagination. I'll discuss more for specific parties here and there. It doesn't matter if you send adorable purchased invitations, create original homemade invitations, or call everyone personally. Just get to it.

I've found that the RSVP (Respondez sil vous plait) on written invitations is often ignored and has to be followed up with a phone call anyway, so I just skip the first procedure. And the phone call gives me a chance to catch up with people I haven't talked to in a while.

It would be unusual to sit down, dial your friends, reach them all and find out on the spot if they are free for your event. Most of the time, these days, you will find yourself leaving a message on their answering machine. You will either tell them why you are calling, with full particulars or ask them to call you back ASAP regarding an upcoming party.

How Not To Do It

Don't make the mistake of saying,

"Hi, this is K, I'm giving a party Saturday, can you come? Call me and let me know."

That invitation allows people to call you when they get around to it (which could be Friday) and doesn't define the party as clearly as this:

11

"Hi, it's K. Gee, I wish you were home. I'm putting together a party for Saturday night. We're going to have dinner and play Pictionary, we're starting at 7 and I expect we will play 'till 11 or so. Could you let me know by Tuesday night at the latest? I'll be home tonight and all morning on Monday. Leave word on my machine if I'm not around. Here's my number, in case you don't have it handy: 123-4567. Hope you can come."

Be sure to have all the party details (time, place, when you need to hear from them, etc.) on a list in front of you while you are leaving the message so you won't overlook anything.

It's important to use the same scenario in person. Be clear about what is going to happen and when. Also, be articulate concerning when you need to have their commitment. I hate planning a party, issuing invitations to people, and still having to track them down the day before the party. If you give people a deadline they can usually manage to take a moment, make a decision and call you.

Fax invitations, of course, are in.

Whatever method you use for sending invitations, plan to follow-up with phone calls a day after the invitation arrives and find out who is coming, so you'll know who to plan for.

Costumes

Costumes are a fun part of any party, but require a huge commitment from the guest. Unless it's a really important party, or Halloween (which cries for a costume), asking guests to come in a complicated disguise might dissuade some from attending. That's why minimal costumes (having people come with their feet "dressed" as Famous Feet or just one piece of clothing to suggest a character) might have a better success rate.

Asking someone to come as his favorite movie star, president, etc., doesn't require the expenditure of time, money and imagination that a Halloween costume might.

Whenever you invite people to come in costume, make it clear there will be people dressed with the most minimal effort as well as quite complicated get ups.

All it takes is one successful costume experience (or really big prizes) for guests to be willing to commit themselves to future projects wholeheartedly.

Games

The same is true of games. For guests who are not accustomed to game playing, there will be many eyes rolling heavenward as you begin to explain the rules. Once committed, however, those same guests will leave telling each other it was the most wonderful party they ever attended.

Surprise!

I happen to be one of those people who *loves* surprise parties. I am somewhat in the minority, it turns out. Some people, of course, say they hate surprises and are charmed by them anyway. But, make sure you know who you are dealing with.

First of all, if you are going to surprise someone, find some way to make sure she is going to look great even though it's a surprise. It's no fun to be the ugliest person at the party. If your hair looks terrible, your socks don't match, or you never got around to shaving, it won't be fun no matter how much effort the party giver went to.

If you live with the surprisee, make sure guests can RSVP to some other number so that you are not getting all kinds of mysterious calls that make the guest of honor either feel left out or suspect you are having an affair.

If you do pull off a real surprise, as soon as your victim is surprised, get the party going on to whatever the event is other than surprising. Otherwise the surprisee just kind of stands there saying, *"My goodness. My goodness. I never suspected a thing. Can I have a chair?"* or other equally intelligent repartee.

If the person is elderly, you might stand alongside saying things like: *"There's Mary Green over there. Doesn't she look great?"* or *"Tom Green, I'm so glad you could come."* As a matter of fact, I wish someone would stand next to me all the time and do that. I can't remember names *or* faces. I think my brain is just too full.

Be Clear about the Time

Guests sometimes get confused about time. Many people invite company for 8 p.m. and don't really want or expect them until 9 p.m. Not me. If I say 7:30, I mean it. I let my guests know to come on time. Not only am I very clear about it when I issue the invitation, but from their experiences at my home they have learned I serve dinner within 30 minutes of the time my guests are expected. Always.

When someone is going to be late, and they call, I will hold off making my final cooking arrangements to accommodate them, if I can. If not, I'll just say, *"We may go on without you, but there will be plenty here for you when you arrive. It's okay. Don't worry."*

There have been emergencies when I have been unavoidably late for a dinner party. I always call the hostess and urge her to go ahead without me. I prefer to join a meal in progress, rather than make the guests cranky and ruin their meal by forcing them to wait for me.

Short of an earthquake, an excuse is just that, an excuse. Let everyone get on with the eating.

Curfew

In theory, it's nice to have a party where people are having such a great time they never want to go home, but it's also nice to have people leave before you want to throw them out.

I've been to lots of parties where I was, in fact, ready to leave, but felt I didn't want to bear the responsibility for breaking up the party. Why not set down clear ground rules instead of just yawning and putting on your nightclothes?

It's much more civilized to take a group vote. If you are playing a game requiring the full count of guests, find out everyone's commitments. If some people have baby-sitters or early morning meetings, a poll can be taken and a decision made.

"Let's play until 10:00 p.m. and then have dessert." It's okay for hosts to have early morning appointments, too. Be sure to declare it in advance. No one will mind, because they don't want to overstay their welcome. We all appreciate knowing in advance when it's time to call it a night.

Creature Comforts

Furniture arrangement and lighting are important in making your guests comfortable. Although it is romantic and flattering (the wrinkles don't show) to converse with someone by candlelight, too little or too much light can be really annoying. The worst is "backlighting" where the light source comes from behind the person you are talking to. You are squinting toward a silhouette and wondering why you can't just be good humored about being so ill at ease. Little things make all the difference; if the sun is going down on one side of the room, rearrange the furniture north and south. Group furniture to provide small conversation clusters here and there. Eight people do not converse well together. Seatings of three or four work best.

The First Guest

Being or entertaining the first guest can be uncomfortable if you don't plan for it. If you *do* plan for it, it can be fun for both of you. I like to leave an easy chore undone and enlist the first guest to help me like setting out the glasses, opening the wine or putting the fresh squeezed orange juice in a beautiful pitcher. This gives me something to do with the first guest other than tell them how great they look and it gives the guest a chance to feel useful. When the second guest comes, the first guest is enlisted to show him where to stow his coat, give the house tour, or explain the evening's "game plan".

Walking Into A Crowd

I find it disconcerting to arrive at a party, be greeted by the host and immediately introduced to a roomful of strangers. The best scenario is for the someone to greet you, show you where to put your coat, purse, etc., and be given time to acclimate to the place and people for a moment before plunging in. It's nice, at that time, for the hostess to appear, offer a drink and then introduce you into a small group and get a conversation going before she goes on to take care of other guests.

Make the guest comfortable and begin your event as soon as possible. If you don't have to wait for the group to assemble before beginning, start as soon as the first guests appear. By and large, people are mostly uncomfortable when they have time to focus on the fact that they don't know anybody. The event gives them something to do while they unconsciously begin to bond with the other guests.

As the host, you should move from group to group. Hopefully your guests will follow your lead. Be sure to mention similar interests your guests share as you introduce them. This gives their conversation a starting point. Use good judgement, though. There is nothing I hate more than someone introducing me as an actress and going into great detail by reciting all my credits. It's embarrassing and makes me feel put on the spot.

Best would be to give us just enough information about each other to get a conversation started. The host might mention to me that John Smith has a daughter who wants to be an actress and suggest to John that he might want to ask me some questions about how his daughter could get started. Let the guests discover each other on their own.

Unforseen Events

Although it seems unlikely that a guest might end up staying over because his car won't start, it's easier to be charming about it if the idea has already occurred to you. If you live in the country and people have had to travel to get there, it's probably already happened to you. So have clean sheets on the designated "guest bed" if you don't already, an extra toothbrush, and make sure you have some fresh orange juice and croissant or bagels for a quick and easy "bon voyage" in the morning.

House Rules

Smoking

A calm page or two on a passionate subject. If everyone at the party smokes (or doesn't), there's no problem. If, however, there is a mix of both, it is the host's responsibility to make sure the smokers don't spoil the evening for those who do not smoke.

If *you* smoke, it will be easier for you to confront others who do and suggest they smoke outside.

I am a militant non-smoker. I don't allow people to smoke in my home or my car.

Frankly, I don't cultivate smokers as friends. But if one happens to slip through my defenses and I want to invite them over, I explain the situation first,

"I want to invite you to my home for dinner (or whatever), but I'm militantly against being around smoke. I don't allow smoking in my house. Will you be able to be happy taking your smoking breaks outside?"

Most people who smoke are fine about restricting themselves, if they know about it in advance. My smoking friends think I am weird and make little jokes about me, but they don't smoke in my house. Frequently, non-smoking guests accompany them for their smoking breaks. When planning the guest list, I usually plan my smokers all for the same party so they'll have someone to grouse with.

It always takes courage for me to bring it up. I want people to like me and don't want to say anything that will offend them. As with most things, however, the reality of the confrontation has always been much milder than any of my fantasies. With information coming out daily regarding the hazards of smoking, not only for the smokers but for those inhaling second-hand smoke, it is not only easier to bring it up but more and more people understand.

Drinking

Not only is it the host's moral duty to make sure a guest does not leave his home and drive a car if he has consumed too much alcohol, but in many states (California, for one) it is also against the law.

With this in mind, temper the amount of liquor you provide. Furnish many alternatives. Stop pouring alcoholic beverages after a certain hour and switch to coffee or tea.

Make a game of it, but be clear that you are serious. Give each drinker a pencil and paper and have the imbiber write his signature every thirty minutes. As guests witness the deterioration, they might actually make contact with how much their reflexes are being impaired. Also, this provides an accurate count of drinks consumed. More than one per hour is too many.

Drugs

Drugs, drinking, and smoking all fall into a similar category. It's not up to the host to legislate guests' lifestyle and moral choices. What you decide on this issue is your affair. If you are into excess, you will probably have similar friends. The important thing is that you do not need to feel that you must be polite if a guest oversteps the boundaries. A guest who is "using" when others are not is probably going to make the other guests ill at ease. It is up to you to ward off the problem in advance, if possible. If you know your friend is a substance abuser, you might not want to include him in the first place. If you do want to include him, state the house rules at the time of the invitation. Say you would like to invite him to a party, but the house rules are NO DRUGS and ask if he can abide by that. If not, make some other arrangements for socializing with that person.

If someone uses anyway, quietly ask if you can see them in the other room and ask him to leave. Don't make a big deal out of it. Let him leave by a side door, no need for a group goodbye.

Even though it is important to be flexible about guests' behavior, the limit is reached when their actions make others (you, too!) uneasy.

Reminders

Even though there is a lot of flexibility surrounding any party, there are some truths that bear remembering.

Rules for Hosts

1. Plan a synergistic guest list.
2. Be clear when you issue invitations and follow up.
3. Be conscious of the guests' timidity about costumes.
4. Plan for the first guest and the overnight guest.

5. Warn smokers of house rules at time of invitation.
6. Same thing with drugs.
7. Be responsible about liquor.
8. Keep guests busy. Let them help.
9. Don't be caught unawares. *Plan. Plan. Plan*
10. Be sensitive about surprise parties.

10 Basic Rules for Guests

1. Respond to invitations promptly and definitively.
2. Don't inflict your smoking on others.
3. Be cool with the liquor.
4. Be appreciative of how much time and energy your host has invested.
5. If you bring flowers, offer to arrange them.
6. Although it's nice to bring wine or dessert, a nice bottle of expensive olive oil or fruited vinegar is also a treat.
7. If you must leave early, notify the host in advance and make arrangements to leave quietly without a group goodbye that will break the momentum of the party.
8. Find out the party time parameters when you accept the invitation so you won't overstay your welcome or break up the party before the host intended.
9. If you must be late, *call* and no matter what the hostess says, tell her to *start eating*.
10. Act as though you are at home. If it's hot, open a window. If it's cold, close the door. Be available to help the host. Call before you leave home and ask the hostess if she forgot anything that you can pick up on the way.

Fun Things: The Environment

Some people's homes just "feel good." You step across the threshold and the air changes. You're glad to be there. It's not because the room looks like the front page of House Beautiful, but because the atmosphere reflects the ease with which life is lived in the space. The couch is not so full of color coordinated pillows that there is no room to sit. Instead, it looks so comfortable you just want to grab a book and nestle in. There's a footstool, a swing on the front porch. There are great looking magazines, pictures on the refrigerator door, and delicious left-overs inside. In short, a user-friendly environment.

Lighting

Frequently people give no thought at all to lighting, yet we are all very much affected by it, frequently on an unconscious level. On Broadway, lighting designers are called in to create mood and heighten events by selective illumination. Comedy scenes played in somber light won't get the laughs they do on brightly lit stages.

An actress friend of mine, Sascha Von Scherler, tells a story of her youth. During previews of a new Broadway comedy, she was feeling quite successful for she was getting lots of laughs. More even than the well-known star. As she left the theater one evening she found the stage technicians changing some lighting. *"Oh, what are you doing?"* asks Sascha. *"The star wants some changes,"* said the technicians. There was a moment of awkwardness before they answered her quizzical look with, *"She's having us unscrew all the lights on your side of the stage."*

Dim lighting is not always bad, it's too somber to promote laughter. It's not necessary to have searchlights; you don't want to make anyone look any older than she is. Just provide nice comfortable lighting.

If the evening includes activities that require reading, make sure to have good lighting available for the "old folks" over 40. There's nothing worse than trying to read Trivial Pursuit cards in dim light. Some people have owl-like vision. Not me.

Take care of simple creature comforts. Make sure the temperature is comfortable. If you've planned an outdoor party and a cold spell came through, bite the bullet and bring your guests inside. Don't make them suffer for nature's rudeness. If you do continue outdoors because it's not *that* bad, have shawls and sweaters *out* and in clear sight so that guests don't have to feel uncomfortable asking for protection. If you are outdoors and it's way too hot, provide for shade and plug in a few electric fans on the patio to at least blow the hot air around.

Make it clear where the guest bathroom is located. Make sure you have a fresh roll of toilet paper in the dispenser and an extra in a nearby cabinet.

This is the one room in the house that should look like no one uses it. The last item before guests arrive should be a quick check of the bathrooms. Not only should it be scrupulously clean, it should be stocked with everything a guest could possibly need. Items such as aspirin, alka seltzer, pepto bismol, band-aids, dental floss, needle and thread, tampons (make sure they are in clear view in your most visible cupboard) etc. should all be placed conveniently and attractively in clear view.

Now is the time to break out all those little sewing sets and miniature bottles of mouthwash and lint picker-uppers that nice hotel rooms provide. If you don't have a supply of the above, don't fret. Just make tracks to a discount drugstore and buy little bottles of everything that you can replenish for each party.

Replace your normal light bulb with lower wattage so guests don't travel from the subtle lighting of your living room to a police line-up feeling in your bathroom. I keep magazines in a basket. This is also probably the only time I could rationalize buying a current edition of The National Enquirer and other periodicals requiring that little time and/or concentration.

It's also considerate to have a small scented candle burning in the bathroom with a packet of matches. Although expensive, the Rigou candles (pine scent) have the most pungent fragrance of any candles I have ever smelled. They certainly mask unpleasant odor effectively.

Make sure the lock on the bathroom door works so that guests are not anxious about surprise visitors *or* having to call for help in order to exit.

Plan ahead for coats and purses. Let guests know as soon as they arrive where to put things. If you don't, they will wander about looking for a place and guests' belongings will be all over the house. If you have an area you don't want guests to roam in, keep lights off in those rooms and close the doors. Maybe even post a sign.

Although your guests will be your friends, sometimes their guests are unknown to you so don't leave your heirloom broach or any other valuables lying about.

Select suitable music for the group. Elegant candlelight parties are heightened by classical music. I choose Mozart because I feel it adds such beauty. For Sunday morning brunches, I like to play a Gregorian Chant in the background. In nice weather I open the French doors between my flower bedecked patio and living room so that the two become one huge atrium. With the chant floating over a lovely spring morning, it reminds me of the Cloisters in New York. But, if I wanted to liven things up, I'd switch to Simon and Garfunkel and The Mamas and the Papas. This kind of music arouses memories and makes me want to hum along, tap my foot, and smile.

Other musical ideas that might occur to you based on your own interests or the focus of the party are jazz, golden oldies, country, folk, soul, reggae, rap, opera, bluegrass, dixieland, cabaret, Broadway musicals, new age, renaissance, gospel, barbershop quartets, marches, children's music, holiday music, salsa, lambada, movie themes, the list is endless.

Put your musical selections on tape so it requires very little attention once your guests arrive. Music can even be the focus. Have an "Elvis" party. Invite all the guests to come dressed as Elvis, Priscilla or any of his entourage. Hire a DJ to play his records and rent an Elvis movie for the VCR.

It's not necessary to spend a lot of money on special music. Either look through your own collection, go to the library or do a survey of the local radio stations. Most cities have specialized stations that cater to classical music or jazz, golden oldies or rock 'n roll. Just choose the station that complements your party and let it play. If you send a note to the DJ of the specific show you plan to tune in telling him about your party, there's a good chance he will mention it on the air. You'll feel like you have your own personalized radio station.

Volume

There is nothing worse than going to a party and not being able to converse with the person next to you because the music is too loud. What might be great for a dance party is inappropriate as a background for dinner. Remember, the music is there to complement the people and the party.

Decoration Sources

Toy stores, the dime store (are there still any?), and the hardware store are all great places to wander in for decoration ideas. It's always more interesting to me to see everyday useful items converted into table ornaments. Guests are doubly thrilled to see things like clothes pins or wooden spoons, baby bottles, or old fashioned baby bracelets with their names on them, or sea shells, lottery tickets, etc. used in interesting ways.

Party accessories that feature the guests are also fun. Use pictures you took at earlier parties where the guests were present or leftovers from projects they were involved in.

For a baby shower, wrap all the gifts in paper diapers, give each guest a rattle for a favor, buy inexpensive baby-dolls from the toy store; put each guest's name on one and use them for place cards. Get baby pictures of all the guests or at least the guest of honor.

Decorations, Prizes, Favors

Prizes, favors, and decorations need not be expensive for impact. I found some hilarious glasses (spectacles) that cost me 89 cents apiece. They were just little plastic glasses that children might play with. What set them apart was the cardboard inserts behind the plastic lens. These inserts were flesh colored backgrounds with eyes drawn on, kind of like "Groucho-eyes". There were little holes cut in the pupils so you could see out. Everyone looked completely different in them. They look great wrapped in tissue paper as table favors. When people open them and put them on, the whole timbre of the party changes. Everyone begins to laugh and giggle and behave as if they have known each other for years.

I've also used them as prizes at parties and taken them for presents when I've gone to other people's parties. Everyone wants to know where I got them because they can think of 25 people they would all like to give them to. It takes so much diligence to find adorable inexpensive prizes, favors and gifts that I almost never reveal my sources to my friends. If they ask, I just smile enigmatically and say, "The getting place".

I believe in *lots* of prizes. No matter how old we are, we like to have a memento to carry home. Make enough categories of competition that most or all participants get to do that. Remember how much people like to see their names so if at all possible, print or paint their names on the silliest present...even if it's a balloon.

The point is that favors, clever prizes, and decorations are well worth the time and effort in what they add to your party. When talking about particular parties throughout the book, I will make specific suggestions.

Seating

If you're having a sit-down meal, carefully plan who will sit next to whom. It makes a difference. You may not always be able to pair people to create a synergistic experience, but you can certainly forestall boredom by separating people who probably have nothing to say to one another. Arrange the seating chart to separate people who came together.

Placecards

Instead of just pointing at people and saying, *"You sit there and you sit there,"* use placecards.

There are many possibilities. Lottery tickets are fun to use and might even be lucrative.

Buy placecards or make your own out of construction paper, plain cards from the stationery store, fabric, wallpaper, paper towels or my favorite: acetate. Acetate is the clear stiff plastic that covers most driver's licenses. Use it solo by writing on it with Magic Marker or in combination by covering any of the above. Pressed flowers are fabulous enclosed in acetate with a message scrawled across the front and can be used for placecards or for invitations. Use white, clear-drying glue to bond two clear sheets with flowers, shapes, and/or notes in between.

Playing cards with each guest's name written across the face of them are simple. If you have a **Batman Party,** you can use all Jokers. Other suggestions for placecards include old Christmas cards, postcards, baseball cards, children's large puzzle pieces, telephone message pads, front covers of old paperback novels, photo in a clothes pin, votive candles with guest's name, seed packets, colored post-its cut in shapes (hearts, shamrocks, stars, etc.) balloons with names, decorated eggs, children's mirrors, scrabble tiles spelling out guest's names, legos used the same way, white paper plus crayons at place for drawing but with guest's names already on pad, old wall calendars.

If you have several tables, it's nice to move the guests to different seats for dessert so that they have access to the rest of the guests. A good way to do this is to use place cards that are folded into inverted "V's" with one name on the outside and another name on the inside. At dessert time, everybody turns the cards inside out to find a new name, changes seats and gets to interact with a whole new group of people.

To get the conversation going at the beginning of the meal you might employ The Book of Questions by Gregory Stock (Workman Publishers) for suggestions for table talk.

Don't just pull out the book and begin asking questions. Instead, type a question on each placecard and let the evening take its own shape. The Book of Questions can create heated discussion. You may want to carefully select the questions you use. Another good source for material is The Dictionary of Cultural Literacy by E.D. Hirsch, Jr. and Joseph F. Kett, James Trefil (Houghton Mifflin Publishers). Or get creative and make up your own questions. Actress Millie Perkins poses a good question: *"If you could change careers today and be guaranteed success, what would you do?"* That's provocative.

Table Settings

It's all about style. Paper plates are even okay (though getting ecologically more questionable) if you mix and match colors or write magic numbers on the bottom of each plate and offer prizes for certain numbers, etc. Remind guests to check their numbers before they fill their plates with food.

And for heaven's sake, who said dishes have to match? There's not enough space in my kitchen to hold all the beautiful dishes I covet. So, I routinely buy a place setting of anything that appeals to me and make sure I have *only* one of each thing. My parties end up with an interesting and eclectic look with lots of "oohs and aahhs" over the selection.

I do the same thing with beautiful stemware. I have two or three of this shape and maybe only one of another. I love watching guests compete for my favorite goblet. They've all staked out a particular stem that is "theirs" and they get cranky if someone else uses it. I serve all beverages in stemware because I like the way it looks and think it makes even drinking water an occasion. Because it is not expensive crystal, I don't feel nervous about using it every day. Orange juice and Dr. Peppers both taste better when served from champagne glasses.

If you can make water more appealing just by using a stemmed glass, think of the wonders of using a pink 40 watt light bulb to camouflage old furniture and a needed paint job?

Buffets

Many people prefer to serve from a central eating table where all the food and table settings are laid out ready to go. If you don't have small tables seating 4-8 people for your guests, do provide friendly nooks and crannies where it will be easy to perch and eat. It is pretty impossible to stand and eat real food. Finger food, yes. Real food, no. Anytime you are serving something that must be eaten with a fork or spoon, you need to provide a place to sit down.

Costumes

Even if it's not specifically a costume party, costumes add an added dimension to any gathering. Providing party-particular hats for each guest, t-shirts with names printed on them, paper red/white/and blue vests on the Fourth of July, etc., give your party flair and your guests a lift. Although I mentioned hats and think they are fun, some people just won't wear hats. Guests (male and female) who have spent a long time getting their "look" sometimes find it hard to run the risk of disturbing their handiwork by adding a hat. It's really just as easy to contrive other headgear (funny ears, noses, earrings, etc.) that don't disturb the coiffure.

Environmental Considerations

1. Plan for good weather *and* your worst nightmare.
2. Clean and stock the bathroom.
3. Arrange for hats and coats.
4. Post "off limits" signs if necessary.
5. Plan music.
6. Plan lighting.
7. Make seating plan (if sit-down) or arrange tables and/or trays.
8. Make or buy placecards.
9. Decide which plates, glasses, and silverware to use.
10. Plans favors, prizes, and decorations.

Parties Away from Home

This book is primarily concerned with parties with your home as the setting. But, if you are having folks to a restaurant, a miniature golf course, picnic setting, etc., there are many details to be considered. If you do decide to have the party away from home make sure there's a clean bathroom available. Is parking accessible? Is there going to be another party going on that might interfere? If it's an outdoor activity, is there a bad weather alternative? Are outside heaters available if necessary?

If you are providing the food, is there a convenient place to serve plus a place to wash up afterwards. If others are providing the food, can they handle the number of guests conveniently? Can everyone be served at once? If you are partying at a bowling alley, they may not be able to get hot food to 20 people at the same time. Will it be okay to eat in shifts if necessary?

If they are serving the food, have you done a taste test? Will guests order individually or will you pre-select food for all? Is there a cross-section of beverages and desserts available for those who drink/don't drink and eat sugar/don't eat sugar?

Is there a curfew imposed by the establishment? Do lights go off in the park at a certain time? If you are going to the museum, is there a check room for people's belongings? If the party is at a swimming pool, is there a place to change? Do you need to provide shampoo and dryers? Is there someone available to greet the guests as soon as they arrive, corral them and get them involved in the party immediately? If you are at a restaurant and there are several tables, can you designate various guests to be in charge of particular tables so that you know everyone is being taken care of?

The seating plan, music and lighting are every bit as important as in your home — perhaps more so since you will not be as in control of the time frame so take care to think this through.

Make sure there is a central activity that everyone will be involved in. If you're bowling, arrange a rotation of players so guests get a chance to intermingle. Start the evening with a central gathering in which you assign teams and end with a similar grouping for awards.

Checklist: Parties Away from Home

1. Parking.
2. Bathroom accessibility.
3. Other guests and parties.
4. Bad weather alternatives (heaters/air conditioners).
5. Food availability, preparation, menus.
6. Curfew.
7. Checkroom.
8. Additional hosts.
9. Seating, music, lighting.
10. Central beginning and end.

Fun Things: Food

Ahh! The great equalizer, *food*. Nothing can make people crankier or happier than food. Well, I can think of one or two other things, but I'm concerned here with something we can actually *do* for people. We can't make them more handsome, thinner, or successful, but we can serve delicious appealing food in an appropriate amount of time so that guests don't expect to keel over from starvation or over-drinking while waiting for food.

Years ago in New York, before I was into cooking *at all*, I was having the first ***Ornament Making Saga/Christmas Tree Trimming Party,*** when a guest came in to ask for my white clam sauce recipe. I wasn't even embarrassed to point to the Chef Boyardee can. Now, I'd at least know enough to hide the can and feel guilty.

I don't think my parties were one bit diminished by my lack of food sophistication, but I think they've grown in scope with the addition of great food. I understand now that the effort involved in food preparation comes through to the guests visually, nutritionally and even psychically. (I'm in California, what can I say?)

Though I enjoy the cooking process, I enjoy it more with a helper or two to assist in the final preparations. Whether it's a family member, a friend or a hired gun, it's always a lot more pleasurable and less stressful with help.

Mostly, I like to choose meals that can be prepared in advance and the finishing touches applied at the last minute.

You'll find general and specific recipes in this book. The RECIPES chapter lists those dishes I've put together for my parties that might serve as inspiration for you.

Catering

As far as I am concerned, regular people (of which I consider myself a prime example) mostly don't use caterers. It's expensive and would rob me of one of my most favorite (if harrying) parts of the party preparation. If, however, it is your offspring's wedding, scrape up the funds and have someone else do it. This is an occasion when you are going to be having a nervous breakdown anyway. There is no need to add to your headaches.

If you do decide to hire a caterer, do your research by collecting names over the years when you attend catered affairs that serve food that you like. You can also ask friends, look through the Yellow Pages and/or the local newspapers. Talking to the food editor is really not that difficult. I couldn't believe it when I called one of the food editors of The Los Angeles Times to ask a question regarding a story and the editor actually answered the phone herself!

There are alternatives to catering that are interesting and not so expensive. Obviously, carry-out is an option. If you know of a dish that a particular caterer prepares that you are crazy about and would like to feature at your party, it is possible to ask a caterer to prepare that dish for the number of people you are serving and then just go by and pick it up. Same thing with a nice restaurant that does not normally do "take out". They will usually be happy to prepare a favorite dish en masse and have you pick it up.

Caterers prices vary relative to what tasks you ask them to attend to. Just preparing the food is obviously cheaper than preparing, serving, arranging for tables, chairs, linen, dishes, bartenders, decorations, etc.

It's also possible for you to pre-cook your meal over time and freeze it and hire servers who will attend to last minute preparations plus serve and clean up.

If you are doing a party for Chinese New Year, it's perfectly permissible to buy carry-out Chinese Food and re-heat and transfer to your own serving pieces, etc. If you are going to do this, make sure you call ahead, tell them what you want and when you want it. Don't try to have it delivered at the last minute and serve it hot when delivered unless you're having a poker party or something so informal where everyone will just grab a container, carry it to the table and eat.

There are many different ways to offer food: sit-down, buffet, picnics, a cook-along, desserts only, snacks only, cocktails, brunches, teas, whatever. My personal preference is for real food. I hate desserts only. Today, people are so health conscious that it seems mean to encourage everyone to just indulge themselves. At least give them a chance to eat some real food first. I feel the same way about snacks. People come to these parties and they are usually hungry (who has a real dinner *before* a party?) They end up stuffing themselves on potato chips, cheese dip and celery. They arrive home feeling unsatisfied even if they can no longer walk, and end up going straight to their refrigerator.

Beverages

More and more people are switching from hard liquor to wine. Even more people are opting for Perrier and other interesting fizzy water, so when you set up your "Bar", it should be clear that this bar serves interesting alternatives. My experience has been that except for a few closeted alcoholics, most people are amenable to whatever you are serving. Too many beverage alternatives is kind of like staring for hours at the selection of toilet paper in the grocery store and choosing white after all. That's why I provide red and white wine at dinner parties along with fresh squeezed orange juice, an assortment of sodas (diet and real) and sparkling water. At least 75% choose regular or sparkling water. As I mentioned earlier, I serve all beverages in stemmed glasses, so even the water drinkers feel they are having a "social experience" and can toast with everyone else.

Although sometimes I set up a special beverage center with an ice bucket, glasses, and beverages, most of the time I just serve from the refrigerator. My glasses are stored adjacent to the fridge and the ice is in the icemaker. For those of you with ice dispensers through the door, it is even easier. If you are going to get a keg of beer, do yourself a favor and put it over the sink and spare your floor.

Because I have "participatory" guests, they frequently get their own drinks. A newcomer will be served the first time and encouraged to "be at home" and help himself to refills.

As I'm sure you've noticed by now, I have a real thing about participation. I am really uncomfortable when I go to someone's house and they wait on me all the time. If they have help, that's different, but I feel that I don't want the host to be fetching and carrying for me all evening.

It would discourage me from ever entertaining if I had to spend the whole evening waiting on everyone. If I get to help at my friend's home, or be helped at mine, I find it allows all of us to be more comfortable. Any task is fun if there is company. Well, maybe not childbearing, but you know what I mean.

When to Serve the Food

Everyone has his own taste about how he wants his party to progress. As I mentioned earlier, I serve food within 30 minutes of the time specified for arrival with the invitation. I do this for many reasons. First of all, I think that at 7:30 or 8:00 p.m. (or 11:30 of a Sunday morning) people are ready to eat. Secondly, it makes people relax more as they begin to break bread together. Thirdly, no matter how much I plan, I don't feel able to be "off duty" until the food is served. I am responsible for feeding these people and keeping the evening on some kind of schedule. Once the food is in process, I feel able to relax. I can now turn all my attention toward interacting with my guests and having fun.

I also don't serve hoer d'oerves because I don't want people filling up on other "stuff" which takes the edge off their palates for my main course. And I hate going to parties where there is an hour of snack eating and drinking before the main course. No matter how many promises I make myself not to eat "all that other food", I always succumb and end up overeating.

Special Diets

These days, it's always advisable to ask guests when you issue the invitation if there are foods they do not eat and make arrangements to accommodate this before they arrive.

If every menu you plan accommodates vegans (those who eat no animal products at all including eggs and dairy), there will be a contingent that will leave feeling unsatisfied. It is possible to plan side dishes that are interchangeable and have two main courses. If you were serving pasta, for instance, it would not be difficult to serve two different sauces that would end up making everyone happy. Vegetables are pretty safe (if you don't serve them with a cheese sauce) and so are salads (without eggs). It's all a matter of considering the guests and being creative. The chapter entitled RECIPES at the end of the book will give you some ideas for these events.

Mostly, we end up entertaining people with our own beliefs and tastes so the food is not a problem. Other elements to consider include low cholesterol, low sodium, no sugar, recovering alcoholics (no desserts with liqueurs), Kosher and Seven Day Adventists. Seven Day Adventists don't eat shellfish nor combine meat and dairy at the same meal (or cooked in the same kitchen).

It's not fun being a vegetarian at a weenie roast. Make sure there are vegetables to roast or grill. Delicious!

Food is so personal. Don't deprive anyone of the group eating experience. Although people with different eating habits are used to being good sports about it, imagine how pleased they will be that you made the effort to think ahead and provide something particularly for them

When Guests Bring Food

You can only ask close friends to bring food. If you want to organize an ongoing party where participants all bring food, kick if off with an event at your place where you do everything. Then, the option of everyone bringing food will be discussed and it won't come off as your idea. At that point, be very specific about how the food is to be organized. Who will be the clearing house to make sure you don't end up with either all desserts or all broccoli.

Guests frequently ask what they can bring when you invite them to a party. Some people routinely say, *"Oh, nothing. Just bring yourself."* The person who asks is probably still going to bring something so you may as well say what you want if you have a preference. If you are not an experienced selector of wines, you might say... *"Gee, I'm so bad at picking wine that if you brought a bottle, that would really take a weight off me."* If there's anything you always run short of...ice, bread, lemons, mention it. Give it some thought before they ask so your mind won't just go "tilt" as mine does without preplanning.

1. If possible get at least "last minute help". If you have kids or a husband to help...you're covered.
2. Make it easy for people to wait on themselves.
3. Don't serve anything so complicated that it's going to make you crazy.
4. Serve *soon*. Lots of hoer d'oerves just fill up your guests and ruin the impact of your main course.
5. Remember, waiting too long before serving the food encourages guests to drink too much.
6. Check for special diets when you issue invitations.
7. Make it okay for your guests to eat as sparingly as they wish.
8. Try to serve meals with enough side-dishes to satisfy a vegetarian even if the main course is meat or fowl.
9. Have a list ready when guests say, *"What can I bring?"* Encourage at least one guest to call as they are leaving the house and ask, *"What did you forget?"*
10. If a guest turns up at the last minute with flowers that need to be arranged and you don't have time (why ever would you?), say, *"Golly, they're beautiful. Let me give you a vase. Would you put them in water for me?"*

Traditional Holidays

2   Traditional Holidays

I'm starting the party listings with parties you already know about and may already celebrate your version of. No use throwing you into *National Crayola Day, National Tap Dancing Day,* and others listed under Traditional Holidays until you've at least gotten your feet wet.

Chinese New Year's Party

Chinese New Year is a four-day celebration occurring between January 21 and February 19. The exact date changes from year to year, like Easter. Ever since I saw "Flower Drum Song" 700 years ago, I wanted to go watch an authentic Chinese New Year's Parade. After missing the event all the years I lived in New York (where inevitably CNY is on the coldest day of the year), I finally went to a Chinese New Year's Celebration in Chinatown in Los Angeles. Somehow it wasn't the same without France Nuyen and Jack Soo singing and dancing, but it was still fun. It's a fun way to celebrate another New Year and get a taste of Chinese culture at the same time.

Event

If you live in a city that has an area where Chinese people congregate, you can gather a group, meet for Chinese food and go watch the parade. If you don't have that option or want to stay home, you can put together your own celebration. Play Chinese Charades (use titles like "Charlie Chan and the Purple Tomb," "Chinatown," "The Last Emperor," "The China Syndrome," Confucius sayings: "*If everyone dislikes it, it must be looked into,*" and made up truths: "If you don't clean up plate, it is harder to do dishes." Visit your local library for a book of Confucius quotations. Play charades keyed to the current animal year. 1992 is the Year of the Monkey. Film titles "Monkey Business," "Tarzan and the Ape Man," and "Gorillas in the Mist" as well as sayings like, *"Don't Monkey Around," "I'm going ape over you," "Don't make a monkey of yourself"* and that swell old song, "Gorilla My Dreams" are all ideas to get you started.

A friend of mine gave me a wonderful present, a tin of fortune cookies that had questions in the cookies instead of fortunes. It was really a version of Trivial Pursuit. For this party, stuff your own cookies with trivia questions pertaining to monkeys and/or China.

When I used my Trivial Pursuit Cookies, I just had a regular dinner party and after dinner, while we were all sitting around the table, I passed the tin around. Everyone took a cookie and waited his turn to question the other guests. It was fun for everyone to try to figure out the answer. An answer card came with the questions. When you prepare the questions, you can prepare the answer card as well.

If you don't feel up to preparing the cookies yourself, there's a wonderful company called *Fabulous Favorites* that produces a terrific party helper called "Fabulous Fortune Brownies." Not only are the brownies really terrific and special (there are several varieties) but each brownie has a tailor-made fortune inside.

There's an 800 number (1-800-869-0822). When you order the brownies, you either tell them the fortune you want in each brownie or give them details about the guests and they will custom make the messages for your guests. They send them next day UPS. The fortunes are packaged in Chinese food containers and presented beautifully. They are expensive but well worth it.

At the end of the evening, give guests a lighted sparkler (be careful!) to light the way to the car. Tell them it's a Chinese custom. Who will know?

People

Any number. If you want to send "hard copies," visit the Chinese area of your town or consult a local university for Chinese scholars and ask how much it would cost to have one invitation written for your party in Chinese. Then have it photocopied. Put an English translation on the back. Include a tiny firecracker in the envelope. Placecards are another area where you can use Chinese writing. It shouldn't be too expensive to have your guest's names written in Chinese characters.

Environment

First order of the day is to find out whether the new year will be *"The Year of the Dog," "The Year of the Pig,"* or whatever animal is due up next. There are twelve animals in the Chinese rotation. I've made a list for you at the end of this party write-up. With this information, you have the option of featuring the current animal in decorations, food, etc. If it's The Year of the Goat, decoration and party possibilities range from pictures of

Charlie Brown (who always thinks he's "the goat"), Los Angeles Rams memorabilia, etc. to traditional Chinese lanterns, chopsticks, firecrackers, maps, etc.

Food

Obviously you'll want to serve Chinese food (yours or carry-out) and fortune cookies. Don't overlook the fact that you can buy fortune cookies and stuff your own fortunes in them. It's a little extra trouble but you can tailor the fortunes for your group. If your city has a Chinatown and a fortune cookie factory, you can take your fortunes to them and they will bake them into the cookies for you.

Time

Make up fortunes or trivia. Buy cookies, apples, favors, carrots with greenery, chop sticks, Chinese incense, firecrackers. Make "Confucius sayings" placecards, sparklers. Stuff cookies with fortunes.

Special Notes for this Party

Call library for this year's exact date.

Year/Animal

1992   The Year of the Monkey

1993   The Year of the Rooster

1994   The Year of the Dog

1995   The Year of the Pig

1996   The Year of the Rat

1997   The Year of the Ox

1998   The Year of the Tiger

1999   The Year of the Rabbit or Hare

2000   The Year of the Dragon

2001   The Year of the Snake

2002   The Year of the Horse

2003   The Year of the Sheep or Goat

▶ Valentine's Day

Valentine's Day is traditionally a time when couples celebrate alone. While they are out there being "alone together," there are a lot of happy singles (like myself) who feel out of place with no one to make a Valentine for. Why not a party that doesn't demand a partner and where everyone has a good time laughing and being silly? The *Valentine Making Contest* party fills the bill on all counts.

Valentine Making Party

Event

This party is best held *before* Valentine's Day so there's still time to send the finished product to some happy recipient. When you post the areas of competition (most beautiful, most humorous, most disgusting, worst taste, best taste, most creative, most traditional, most earnest, meanest, sweetest, sickest, slickest, sappiest, whatever, you will inspire your artists to unthought of highs (and lows). For prizes, use Valentine candy, magic kissing powder (use baby powder or corn starch and manufacture a new label), Love Pills guaranteed to make the object of your affection hopelessly smitten with you (put red hots in a spice bottle and create the label), and Power Drops (put pink-tinted water in a spice bottle, label it and include an eye dropper). Tie all these bottles with lace and/or red ribbon. Use ivory-colored paper and brown ink
for a sepia-tinted antique look.

People

Eight or more. Use bought or homemade valentines for invitations. Include candy hearts, red hots or paper hearts in the envelope for added flair. Avoid messy spills by writing on the envelope: *"Careful when opening. Tiny treats inside."*

Environment

Decorate with lots of lace, hearts, red ribbons, and old valentines. For music search out titles with the word "love" in them: "I'd Love to Get You on a Slow Boat to China,"

41

"Love Makes the World Go Round," "Do You Love Me?," "Indian Love Call," etc. When guests arrive, hang a red satin ribbon with a heart on it around their neck or encourage them to wear their heart on their sleeve. Make the heart from quilted fabric, wire, pipe cleaners, twisted ribbon, etc.

Food

I get romantic around Valentine's Day and want everything to be really pretty and very pink. Serve pink heart-shaped ravioli filled with pureed pumpkin, eggplant or other vegetables. Use traditional meat or cheese fillings, if you prefer. For dessert, serve pink-tinted flan or creme caramel. For non-sugar eaters like myself, serve strawberry yogurt on a crisp flour tortilla and add a few sliced strawberries for a "Fruit Taco." Serve dinner buffet-style allowing guests to wander among the art, eat and judge all at the same time.

Time

Assemble supplies for Valentines: papers, fabrics, glues, scissors, etc. Make necklaces of red ribbons and hearts, hearts for sleeves, magic potions, love drops, powders. Have work spaces ready with construction paper, laces, velvets, sequins, feathers, ribbons, nuts, bolts, scissors, glues, glue sticks, everything you have on hand and that seems a Valentine possibility. Include markers, paint brushes, Q-Tips, crayons, etc.

Special Notes for this Party

Be sure to have the artists sign and display their work.

► Famous Lovers Party

One Valentine's Day, when I was madly in love, I gave a hilarious party where everyone came dressed as a famous lover. It still embarrasses me a little as my love and I came as Adam and Eve with a very few fig leaves painstakingly cut from dark green velvet and placed not as strategically as I had thought at the time. Fortunately the photos no longer exist. Other more conservative, less creative and more comfortable souls came as Elizabeth Taylor and Richard Burton, Sonny and Cher, Elvis and Priscilla, Anthony and Cleopatra, Madonna and Sean, Donald, Marla and Ivana, Casanova, Scarlett and Rhett, Mae West, etc. Not all guests were couples. The inventive singles came as Bluebeard, Cupid, Mickey Rooney, Marilyn Monroe, etc.

If you don't want to have guests don costumes, you can still have a Famous Lovers Party by putting signs on them when they arrive, but it's a lot fun to come in disguise.

Event

Not only do you get to dress up as your favorite lover at a *Famous Lovers Party* (oh, man, I'm dying to come as *Cher!*) but, it's a great excuse to act like your role model as well. Play *Famous Lovers Who Am I?* When the guest arrives, the host pins a sign with a famous lover's name on it to the guest's back. The other guests, of course, can read the sign.

In order to find out who you are, you ask questions that can be answered "yes" or "no": "Am I living?" "Am I a writer?", etc. You can only ask two questions of the same person and then must move on and ask someone else. Once everyone is acquainted move onto dinner and then prepare for the main event: *The Love Poem Contest.*

Have a work space with paper and pencils and romantic items like old love letters (phony, of course), pressed flowers and faded pictures for inspiration. Everyone draws the name of another guest to whom he must write an anonymous four-line love poem. Assignments are uni-sex so it doesn't matter if you end up writing one to your Aunt Matilda if you invited her. The unsigned poems go into a hat. They can either be addressed to "The woman in the appealing green sweater" or "To Mary."

When all are finished, each guest pulls out a poem, reads it and everyone guesses who wrote it. Prize possibilities include tiny books of poetry, a pot of any small red flowers, baby's breath, violets, red tulips, Forget Me Nots or seeds or bulbs for the above. Other ideas include anything romantic: scented soaps, red helium-filled balloons, and if you are feeling really racy (and the recipient would see the humor) give red condoms! Give prizes for most sentimental, cleverest, most succinct, most unusual, most colorful, most proper, etc. The more original categories you think of, the more you will not only inspire your poets, but the more prizes you can give.

Guests

Eight or more - dressed as famous lovers. Use homemade or store-bought valentines for invitations. Include candy hearts, red hots or paper hearts loose in the envelopes. Write on the outside of the envelope a warning to open carefully. Nothing cools enthusiasm as quickly as having to sweep up someone else's clever idea off the floor.

Environment

Decorate with lace, red ribbons, lots of hearts and any old valentines you might have that are not too personal. Forge love-letters of famous people: *"Not tonight, Josephine"* and sign it with a big "N" for Napoleon. Perhaps, *"Darling, I really 'give a damn'"* and sign it "Guess Who?" Write the notes on romantic paper and either put them on the wall or leave them scattered around on tables. Frank Sinatra's "Songs for Swinging Lovers" would be perfect to set the theme for the evening. Then seque into old movie love themes. All are available on "Golden Oldie" compilations.

Food

Serve Chinese Chicken Salad or a rare Chateaubriand. For vegetarians, make a vegetable loaf in a heart-shaped mold. Oysters or some other known aphrodisiac will add zest to the table.

Serve beets and cut them into heart shapes with a cookie cutter. Or mash potatoes with a bit of red food coloring to tint them pink and pipe through a pastry bag into the shape of hearts. Have a salad featuring red lettuce. For dessert, consider a red gelatin mold with candy hearts inside. Be sure to make a non-sugar version, if possible.

Don't serve *everything* red, just here and there with other colors for balance. See the RECIPES for more detailed Valentine food instructions.

Time

Gather paper, pencils, fountain pens, markers, pressed flowers, sachets, plus inspirational material (pictures of Clark Gable, Rudolph Valentino, Marilyn Monroe, Garbo, etc.)

Special Notes for this Party

Save time for writing phony love letters of famous people.

► **President's Day**

February is a patriotic month. You can celebrate Washington's Birthday complete with cherry pie and hatchets or you can go for Honest Abe and Lincoln Logs for you-know-who.

Lincoln's Birthday Party

Lincoln's birthday is February 12, but is celebrated on the closest Monday. Stage a Lincoln party by firelight and candlelight. Since that's all Lincoln had
to study by, it should get everyone into the mood of things.

Event

Lincoln's Birthday is a fabulous day when you can feature red, white and blue everything from decorations to food. Give guests fake beards to wear and play *Lincoln Charades:* The Gettysburg Address, *"Four score and twenty years ago,"* "The North and South," "Lincoln," or make up a *Lincoln Trivia* game asking questions like: *"What famous mountain features a likeness of Lincoln?" (Mt. Rushmore), "Lincoln rose to prominence through a series of famous debates. Who was his opponent?" (Stephen A. Douglas), "How long was Lincoln president before the Civil War began?" (One month.)* Take a trip to the library for more information. Use pennies or Lincoln Logs for prizes.

People

Eight or more. If you want to send invitations rather than call, enlarge and color photocopy a five-dollar bill (which features Abe, of course), coat the copy with acetate and write party particulars in red marker across the acetate.

Environment

Candlelight and/or firelight will give a nice cast to this party. Since Lincoln was a lawyer, old law books (visit a second hand book store) scattered among American flags and red, white, and blue streamers will add ambience. Get a copy of "Battle Hymn of the

Republic," "The Star Spangled Banner," and "America the Beautiful." After the tone has been set for the evening, switch to harpsichord music. You can get an inexpensive tape of harpsichord music at a good record store. (Do we still say records now that it's all tapes and CDs?)

Food

Turkey with cranberry sauce is a good possibility. Many people don't remember to serve turkey except at Thanksgiving and Christmas. A pretty and delicious vegetarian pasta with fresh chopped tomatoes, garlic, olive oil and fresh basil or red peppers is a great alternative. Strawberry, rhubarb or cherry pie for dessert with vanilla ice cream and blueberries. For non-sugar eaters, have a beautiful crystal bowl filled with blueberries and strawberries. This time of year, you'll have to make do with frozen, but it will still be delicious. Have cream whipped without sugar on the side for garnish.

Time

Prepare charade material and Lincoln trivia, arrange for fake beards, plan and prepare food. Make red, white and blue decorations.

Special Notes for this Party

Because color photocopies are so well done, be sure to photocopy the five-dollar bills a little large (or smaller) than actual size so you don't end up in jail for counterfeiting. I happened to be in my bank one day after photocopying some bills for invitations and was showing the teller how well they turned out when the manager walked by. He was *not* happy and told me that what I was doing was illegal. Even though photocopying machines have been constructed so that they cannot make an exact copy (size-wise), make sure there is no question and add or subtract 1/8 of inch to your copies.

Washington's Birthday Party

Event

Washington's birthday is February 22, but, is celebrated on the Monday closest to that date. Your party can take place anytime from February 15 until the 22nd. For a Washington's Birthday party, give guests little colonial flags or tiny hatchets on ribbons to wear around their necks. Alternate using red, white and blue ribbons. Since it's the old truth-teller's birthday, what better event than playing "Dictionary" or "Balderdash?" These are both clever games that call for lying.

For "Dictionary" give everyone a paper and pencil. One person takes the dictionary and chooses a word that he feels most people will not know the meaning of. He announces the word. He spells the word. Each member of the group now has three minutes (or whatever time you determine) to make up a definition for that word and write it down in "dictionary-ese." The person who chooses the word writes the true meaning from the dictionary on his paper.

All papers are folded and put into a hat. The person who chooses the word reads off the definitions one at a time while the others vote on what they perceive as the real definition.

Players get five points for guessing the correct definition and one point each for every time someone votes on his incorrect definition as the Real McCoy.

"Balderdash" is a store-bought game available at most toy stores. It also involves tall-tale-telling, but you need a game board to play it.

Prize possibilities include a teeny tiny dictionary from the dime store, a selection of dictionaries from a second-hand store and/or tiny hatchets from a doll house supply center. If you can find them, give long noses in honor of Pinocchio.

People

Eight or more (hopefully with a sense of history) definitely with a sense of humor.

Environment

For placecards, make color photocopies of one-dollar bills and cover them in acetate (you won't believe how real they look). Make the copies obviously larger or smaller so that no one thinks you are a counterfeiter (really!). Use red magic markers to write the guest's name across the acetate before placing it in the middle of their plate.

Food

In honor of George, why not a colonial dish? Game pie is a possibility. You'll find most of them garnished with cherries, which will fit in with the whole "George" theme. There are directions for "George's Duck" in RECIPES. Cherry cobbler and cherry pie with vanilla ice cream with blueberry topping makes for a patriotic-looking menu. For sugarless dessert, use strawberry, blueberry and vanilla yogurt layered in champagne glasses. Sprinkle Grapenuts here and there and layer with bananas.

Time

Gather paper, acetate, pencils, small flags, dictionary, hatchets, dollar-copies and timer.

Special Notes for this Party

Although the most enduring folklore about George involves the cherry tree, he was a much love and respected president. After his death, he was praised in Congress as, "First in war, first in peace, first in the hearts of his countrymen." A banner wih this slogan would add ambience and conversation to this party.

Additional President Possibilities

If your taste in Presidents runs to more recent history, have a *Nixon Party*. This is a party I was inspired to have because Dick and I share the same birthday (it's so tacky to have a party for yourself). Since our birthdays coincide, I feel close enough to call him Dick. We Capricorns stick together.

Nixon's Birthday Party

Event

I've grouped this party with the other presidents in the name of patriotism, so that you can add a new wrinkle to President's Day and celebrate all presidents if you choose and combine ideas. Actually our birthday is January 9 if you want to be specific. Have guests come as Dick or Pat and at the end of the evening, crown the "best Dick and Pat" and have a birthday cake with candles for all the Dick's to wish for a return to the presidency (or whatever) and blow out the candles. Play *Nixon Who Am I?* and use Kissinger, John Dean, Martha Mitchell, Carl Bernstein, Bob Woodward, etc. After dinner you can play *Nixon Charades:* The Final Days, All the President's Men, Blind Ambition, etc.

For prizes: Paperback copy of All the President's Men, Blind Ambition, or visit your library to find a picture of Martha Mitchell. Photocopy and enlarge it inscribing it *"To (winner's name), You were swell! Love, Martha."*

People

Finally the perfect party for all your Republican friends! Actually this party is fun for people of all stripes (just don't get into any political discussions). Eight or more at this party - the more Dick's the merrier! If you have the time and inclination, the funniest invitations would be to make short tapes for each friend with all the party details. Tell them you are leaving seven seconds of silence in honor of the occasion and that you hope they will record their reply and return it in the next mail. At the party play the tapes all strung together. Mention on your tape that someone may be listening...so be careful.

Visit The International House of Pancakes and ask to borrow one of their menus and see if you can buy a few paper napkins. I went by and talked to one manager and he said he would be happy to give me what I needed.

Photocopy the menu after substituting your name on the cover: "K's House of Pancakes". Hang them about for decoration. Put one over the door to your kitchen.

Food

There are endless pancake possibilities: bananas, blueberries, strawberries, apples sauteed in butter with raisins and cinnamon, etc. Get a companion cook to help you turn out pancakes for the mass production line of pancake extravaganzas.

Provide a salad, a green vegetable and lots of bacon (if it's a meat-eating crowd). For the vegetarians, serve steamed green beans with walnuts with a light vinaigrette dressing.

Time

Plan and prepare food, get menu/napkins, make sign, toy pancake turners, make macaroni necklaces, buy and paint wooden spoons.

Special Notes for this Party

Make sure you have enough griddles for all the pancakes so it doesn't take all night to cook them.

Grammies, Emmies, Tonys, Etc.

I keep looking forward to the year that I will miss this party because I will be at The Dorothy Chandler Pavilion myself draped in sequins and bugle beads ready to pick up my own "Oscar." Until then I'll get to sparkle in my living room at my own Academy Awards party.

Event

The Academy Awards are traditionally held the first Wednesday in March. Many people like to get together to watch the Awards on television. As long as it's a Gala in Hollywood, why not in your living room? Invite guests to come dressed up (or not as they prefer). Give home-made ballots to the guests. Have them vote not only on all the major categories but since, let's face it, part of the fun of watching the event is to "dish" everyone's outfit, vote on Best Dress, Worst Dress, Most Incredible Hair, Most Stupid Interview Question, Most Stupid Interview Answer, Best Acceptance Speech, Worst...etc., etc., make up your own. Have guests fill in the first part before the show begins, turn them over and fill in best/worst dress, etc., as show is in progress. At the end of the show while all are joining in coffee, dessert, whatever, everyone will read his answers. Give prizes for most and fewest correct answers on the formal categories.

People

Any number. When they arrive, drape them in sequins to get into the spirit of the evening. Good fabric stores sell sequins backed with elastic. They are not that expensive and can be wrapped into belts, ties, hats, bracelets, etc. In Los Angeles, there are inexpensive near-replicas of Oscar that make good prizes. If there are none in your city, other options include: a copy of <u>Variety</u> (from any good news-stand - or write <u>Variety</u>, 5700 Wilshire Blvd., #120, Los Angeles, CA 90099-4359), a movie magazine, a copy of <u>The National Enquirer</u>, a star of any kind, a paperback biography of any film star. For the EMMIES give <u>The Complete Directory to Network TV Shows</u>. For a show celebrating the TONYS, give Simon Callow's book, <u>Being an Actor</u>. For the GRAMMY'S, give this year's nominated albums.

Telegrams get everyone's attention, so for a clever touch for this party, why not create your own telegrams? Visit Western Union and get some telegram blanks and use them for invitations. As you know, the Awards are televised so when you inform them of their "nomination", invite them to the ceremonies. Something like,

"Congratulations from the Academy of Motion Picture Arts and Parties: You have been nominated for your performance in "Reversal of Fortune." There will be a private awards ceremony at 1123 Elm St., Anywhere, U.S.A. on February 28, 1990. The awards will begin promptly at 6 p.m. We will begin immediately. Doors will be closed promptly. Don't be late. Formal attire. Dinner will be served. Mary Smith, a representative of the Academy, will be in touch. Please RSVP by February 24."*

*Do variations for the other awards shows.

Follow up with a phone call to answer any questions and make sure the guest is coming and that he understands that any attempt at formal-attire will be accepted.

Environment

Decorate with film posters and headlines from your local newspaper hyping this year's Awards. Visit the library and get copies of last year's paper celebrating those winners.

If you have a small group, watch together in the living room. If you have a larger group, you can spot televisions all over the house and have "watching centers" here and there. If you want to give real panache to the evening, have matchbooks printed:

ACADEMY AWARD
NOMINEE
DATE

Have them printed in silver or gold and spread them around the house. No one will be able to resist taking one of those home.

Food

Serve your favorite buffet with a new twist attaching a star's name to each dish. "Lee J. Cobb Salad," "Sissy Spacek Spinach," "Cybill Shepherd Pie," "Danny DeVito DeVegetables," "Marilyn Monroe Mousse," etc. Encourage guests to help themselves throughout the evening. Serve "Chevy Chase Cheesecake" and champagne after the awards.

Time

Make ballots and sequined favors. Pick up movie magazines, <u>Variety</u>, <u>The National Enquirer</u>, Oscar replicas, and stars. Go to the library for last year's clippings. Buy, plan and prepare food.

Special Notes for this Party

If possible adapt the food to this years nominees, A variation of this party is the *Oscar Party for Two*. A friend of mine dressed in a formal gown, set a candlelight table for two with champagne (complete with ice bucket) and the man in her life arrived in his tux with elegant carry-out. This sounds like something I'd love to do.

* The EMMYS are traditionally held on a Sunday in September although sometimes elections and World Series make August a necessity. The Academy of Television Arts and Sciences' phone number is 818-953-7575, for more specific information. The GRAMMIES are held the end of February, usually on a Wednesday. The Grammy phone number is 213-849-1313. The Country Music Awards

are held in April. They are produced by Dick Clark Productions. Call their offices at 213-659-9101 for more specifics. The TONY Awards for excellence in the New York Theater are traditionally held on a Sunday in June. Further information number is 212-764-1122.

► St. Patrick's Day

When I became old enough to notice that many people use St. Patrick's Day as an excuse to get drunk, I was pretty surprised. Yes, the Irish are known to "take a nip" now and then, but the trait that I find most endearing and interesting is their charm and ability to tell tall tales - and that is far more interesting and civilized than watching everyone fall down.

Event

St. Patrick's Day is March 17 and should be celebrated on that day, week night or not. You and your fellow leprechauns can "Kiss the Blarney Stone" and tell a few Tall Tales. You can even have an *Irish Brogue Contest*.

The Irish myth is "If you kiss the Blarney Stone, all your dreams will come true." It shouldn't be too hard to find a big rock of some kind, put a sign on it and ensure each guest's future happiness by inviting them to give it a kiss. Take a picture to immortalize the event.

People

When you extend the invitation, ask guests to prepare a tall tale and be prepared to tell it around the table after dinner. Give prizes for tallest tale, best Brogue and most believable story. You can even give a prize for red hair and freckles (very Irish). It's always more fun to announce areas of competition on the invitation to stimulate your guests' thoughts for their stories, as well as what they will wear. For prizes, give a bottle of green beer, a green baseball cap, honorary Irish citizenship and long noses if you can find them.

Add "Mc" to the front of the guests' last names on placecards or invitations. Make color photocopies of a one-dollar bill (shrink them to avoid jail terms!) cover with acetate and pin them to guests as they arrive for a different kind of "Wearin' of the Green". Have a bouquet of four-leaf clovers hung over your door. Give everyone a kiss and tell them it's an old Irish custom. Be sure to warn the guests that those who don't wear green on St. Patrick's Day "get pinched".

Environment

There's a cereal called Lucky Charms that has shamrock-shaped nuggets. Have bowls around for nibbling. Decorate with shamrocks, green balloons, green crepe paper, Irish rock n' roll, Irish folk songs, green beer, green baseball caps, honorary Irish citizenship, Celtics or Fighting Irish poster. Music ideas: Irish Rock n' Roll (Van Morrison, U2, Sinead O'Connor, etc.) or Irish Folk Music (Clannad, Irish Rovers).

Food

Serve Corned Beef and Cabbage and "Irishup" Irish potatoes by sprinkling fresh chopped chives all over them.

Time

Rig blarney stone, tape music, get prizes, plan, collect and prepare food, photocopy and acetate money.

Special Notes for this Party

As the prize for "tall-tale-telling," crown the tallest tale teller as the prize to the King and/or Queen of Blarney. Use a wreath of real or paper shamrocks. Give them green shamrock stickers to attach to the foreheads of guests who are being too serious.

▶ April Fool's Day Party

A friend of mine has a great idea for an April Fool's Day Party. When the guests arrive, answer the door wearing a robe, with your hair in curlers and tell them they got the date wrong. Once they are thoroughly confused, holler "April Fool" and invite them in. When everyone has gathered, pull out the curlers, take off your robe (please be dressed underneath!) and proceed to have a wonderful party.

Event

A Foolish Celebration. This is a day ripe for silliness. Just so no one forgets, put guests to work as soon as they arrive creating their own Fool's Cap. You remember all those comic strips with people wearing dunce caps? Well, that's what we're talking about here. Provide construction paper, trimmings and an elastic chin strap to keep the hat from falling off. Turn the event into a contest and give prizes for biggest, shortest, funniest, most intelligent, etc. Give water guns and fake moustaches, phony snakes, and spiders, hand buzzers, squirting flowers for prizes. Play *Foolish Who Am I?* and use names of people you think are foolish: Andrew Dice Clay, Richard Nixon, Gerald Ford, Chevy Chase, Jimmy Swaggart, Donald Trump, Penn & Teller, Foolish Pleasure, etc. Play stupid card games like Spoons, Pig, and Indian.

Spoons

To play spoons, you need a deck of cards, and enough spoons for all but one of your guests. Put the spoons in the middle of the table, spaced in a circle. Deal four cards to each player. The object of the game is to get four cards all alike. Four 3s, 2s, etc. The first player to get four of a kind *quietly* takes a spoon and continues to play. As soon as another player notices a spoon is gone, he may *quietly* take a spoon even if he does not have four of a kind.

This continues until everyone notices and takes a spoon. The person spoon-less loses. Keep score by spelling out A-P-R-I-L F-O-O-L. Each loss gives you one more letter until someone wins/loses the title of April Fool.

The play of the hand goes like this. After dealing, the dealer takes one or more cards off the top of the deck looking for cards that will match something she has in her hand. Remember, she is looking for four of a kind. If she sees a card she wants, she takes it, puts it in her hand and passes the card she replaced *and* the other cards she looked at, face down, to the player on her right. That player does the same as the dealer picks up more new cards and checks them out. The cards continue going around the table until someone gets four of a kind. It's important to keep the cards moving quickly, so that people are so intent on checking their cards that they don't readily see someone taking a spoon. If the dealer runs out of cards before someone wins, she just takes cards from the discards that have come back to her.

Pig

Pig is played the same way, except, instead of taking a spoon when you have four of a kind, you put your forefinger to the side of your nose and keep it there until the game is over. It's stupid and silly and difficult to keep checking out cards and keeping them going with your finger to your nose, but it's lots of fun.

Indian

Indian is a variation of Poker. The dealer deals one card per person *face down*. The players are not allowed to look at their cards. When everyone has his card, the dealer says *"go"* and everyone takes his card *without looking at it* and places it on his forehead facing out so that everyone else can see his card, but he cannot. Then, each player, after looking at everyone else's card, decides to bet (a penny, a match stick, a poker chip, whatever you decide to play with). The highest card wins. Many people look around the table, see a couple of face cards, people sniggering and decide their card must be very low and they drop out without betting. Sometimes they look at their card and find out it would have won, but they have been psyched out by their opponents.

The person to the right of the dealer "opens" by saying *"I'll bet one penny"*, the next person may either decline to bet, bet a penny or decide to raise.

Same principles as poker. When the betting is over, everyone looks at his card and the person holding the highest card wins.

Play this game at least once around the table so that everyone has a chance to deal. Even the most stuffy guest has to forego dignity with a card plastered to the center of his forehead. Be sure to take pictures. This is my favorite silly game.

At the end of the evening, present prizes for dunce caps and also for the winners of the games.

People

As many silly people as you can get in a room all at the same time. Now that may only be four or five as a lot of people take themselves very seriously. No use inviting those folk, this is a party for clever people who are young at heart. If you don't stimulate each of them to pull some dumb trick on the group before the evening is over, it will not be a successful party.

Environment

Decorate with pages from calendars with the wrong date circled. Have lots of trivia on the walls, some of it true, some of it not. Music possibilities include: "What Kind of Fool Am I?", "I'm Just a Fool In Love," "Fool for Love," "Fool on the Run," etc.

Food

Serve non-serious finger food: quesadillas, tacos, pita bread, flour and corn tortillas. Have tuna salad, egg salad, avocados, tomatoes, thinly sliced cucumbers, sprouts and anything else that appeals to you so that guests can concoct their own sandwich. Have sour cream, guacamole and vinaigrette for dressings. For dessert, serve Strawberry Fool, a British concoction made of fruit, scalded or stewed, crushed and mixed with cream. And pickles. I just think pickles are funny.

Time

Assemble construction paper, trim for hats, playing cards, spoons, poker chips, menu and food. Put together the calendar pages. Make up outlandish/truthful trivia. Prepare *Foolish Who Am I.*

Special Notes for this Party

Put pencil and index cards by the front door with a sign that says: *"Please list the three most foolish things you ever did. Be prepared to read this at 10 p.m. (or some time near the end of your party). There will be prizes."*

▶ Easter Party

When I was a little girl, Easter was a time to get new shoes and hunt Easter Eggs. I don't always get new shoes now, but I make it a point to invite guests so I can still hunt Easter Eggs.

Event

It's not fair that kids are the only ones who traditionally get to hunt Easter Eggs. I think one of the reasons that adults can be so cranky is that we passed all the fun things on to the under twelve set. A couple of years ago, my friend Rue McClanahan invited me over for an Easter Egg Hunt. Team A hid eggs for Team B in the front yard while Team B hid eggs for Team A in the back yard. The team that found the most eggs won. There was a fun silly prize for each team member. We started hiding eggs as soon as all the guests had assembled and ate dinner as soon as the last egg was found.

Since Easter is a floating holiday, consult your calendar for the date. It's not necessary to have this party on Easter Sunday. It can take place anytime the week before but it really *does* need to take place in daylight hours. Easter is one of my favorite days for a Brunch with the egg hunt following the food. Plan for good weather but be prepared to hide eggs all over your house if the weather doesn't cooperate.

At Rue's party, eggs were hidden at the bottom of the swimming pool and in the lower eaves of the house. She gave each of us little baskets to carry our eggs in.

When everyone has gathered, draw for teams and begin hiding eggs. Allow 15 minutes for hiding eggs. 30 minutes for finding eggs. Even if all the eggs are not found, the time limit is the time limit. Teams turn in their baskets and eggs for the official count. Prizes are awarded after lunch for all members of the winning team plus the individual who finds the most eggs as well as the one who finds the least. Call it the "Good Egg" award.

People

Eight or more. Any age. Any shape. At Rue's party there was even a wheelchair and he won! If you want to send hard copy invitations, celebrate the rebirth that Easter celebrates by including a packet of seeds in your invitation. Buy four different packs of seeds you like and divide them into smaller packets. Tape four 2x2 envelopes together to make containers for four different kinds of seeds. Write party particulars on one side and planting instructions on the other and use this as the invitation. For prizes, visit a second hand bookstore and find copies of The Egg & I and Harvey. Also get recipe books featuring eggs. For all members of the winning team, possibilities include toy egg timers, compasses or pastel-colored bandannas which you can have printed —

NATIONAL EGG HUNT CHAMPIONS
Date

Egg Toss

An exhilarating game to accompany this is the egg toss. Each guest selects a partner. Each couple begins tossing a raw egg back and forth while standing quite close to one another. After each toss, they take a step back. The couple who can toss the egg farthest without breaking it wins. A suspenseful and sometimes messy game, but lots of *fun*.

Environment

Give everyone a basket as soon as they arrive. Since a lot of this party is to be outdoors, don't forget to decorate the plants and trees with helium-filled balloons and pretty pastel ribbons. Feature music with "Spring" in the title: "It Might As Well Be Spring," "Spring Is Busting Out All Over," "Spring Will Be a Little Late This Year," and of course, "Easter Parade."

Food

Serve cheese souffle, green salad, deviled eggs, and steamed asparagus with a light vinaigrette. For dessert, strawberry parfait pie or yogurt parfaits of blueberry, strawberry and vanilla yogurt layered in stemmed glasses with a few strawberries, sliced bananas and Grapenuts.

Time

Dye at least six eggs per guest, get baskets for everyone. Arrange for balloons and ribbons. Deal with the menu, buy food, buy compasses, and egg timers. Get bandannas printed.

Special Notes for this Party

Either buy grass or make your own by shredding hot pink, green, turquoise, whatever, tissue paper. After all the hunting and counting, it is sometimes difficult to get people to accept responsibility for all those eggs. Have a group "deviled-egg-making-experience", so you won't waste them.

Bonnet Making Contest

If you don't want to hide, hunt or throw eggs or if your party is at night and that seems impractical, here's an alternative.

Event

Bonnet Making Contest/Egg Dyeing Gala. One year I invited about ten adults. We had an Easter Egg coloring and decorating contest as well as an Easter Bonnet Making contest. All manner of art supplies, paper, glue, trims, odds 'n' ends, were assembled on two work tables and the guests were alternately as quiet and as unruly as kindergartners intent on a project. At the end of the evening, everyone modeled his bonnet to the tune of "Easter Parade," while a team of impartial (?) judges selected the wittiest, prettiest, weirdest, best effort gone wrong, etc. and prizes were awarded accordingly. Prize ideas: doll hat boxes, fake certificates for scholarship to millinery school, a copy of Vogue, or any other fashion magazine. Announce categories of competition ahead of time for inspiration or make up the categories after you see the hats so that everyone gets a prize.

People

Eight or more. Either provide them with simple aprons (crepe paper aprons in pastel colors would be great) or encourage them to dress for action. If you want your activity to be a surprise, just tell them to dress casually in something they wouldn't mind getting glue on. If you send invitations, cut pictures out of magazines and newspapers of famous people wearing hats (the sillier the better) and paste them on acetate. Write party particulars across the front with a terrific colored magic marker.

Environment

I decorated the house with pictures cut from fashion magazines of men and women in all kinds of hats and featured a banner, "The Return of the Hat People."

Food

We ate deviled eggs, ham, potato salad, and beautiful young asparagus steamed with a little vinaigrette on the side and sliced tomatoes. For dessert, I made bread pudding.

Time

Assemble art supplies; plan, buy, and prepare food; buy or make prizes, copies of fashion magazines, hat boxes; collect hat people pictures, make banner.

Special Notes for this Party

Take pictures of the evening, particularly of each contestant in her creation. For a real sensation, rig or rent a rabbit costume. All you really need are grey (or pink or white) sweats, some ears, whiskers, and a carrot.

► Derby Day Party

Just because you don't live in Kentucky doesn't mean you can't have a great Derby celebration. One year, my daughter Kelly (horsefan/pumpkin pie maker) convinced me that there was a strike in Kentucky and the Derby was going to be run in New York at the Belmont Racetrack and why couldn't we go? By now, I *know* that come hell or high water, the Kentucky Derby is *always* run at Churchill Downs, but that doesn't keep me from staging my own event at my house.

Event

Mock Derby Race. The Kentucky Derby is run the first Saturday in May. A wonderful excuse for a party whether you want to dress up, drink Mint Juleps and watch the big race on television or just pitch horseshoes in the yard.

Check out the paper ahead of time and note the names and numbers of all the horses in the race so that you can greet each guest, drape him with a banner, and announce that today he is a stand-in for one of the horses running in today's race. Give him $100 in play money and invite him to bet on any guest (horse) he likes. Tell him the guest who picks the winning horse, and the horse that generates the most bets will receive prizes. Guests then go about before the race soliciting bets on themselves. All bets must be in five minutes before post time.

For prizes, give paperback horse books (Come on Seabiscuit, My Friend Flicka, Black Beauty, etc.) For the winning horse, give an apple or carrots with greenery attached.

Also, make a wreath for the winner out of some kind of flowers. You can buy a styrofoam form from a florist supply house. Then just stick flowers and/or greenery into that. The real winner of the Kentucky Derby gets a horseshoe of roses.

Since the race is over very quickly, I suggest lots of horsey activities. Play Horseshoes. Rent a pony and take pictures of all the guests sitting on top of him. Provide a top hat for the men and an organdy flower extravaganza for the ladies for the photo. Give the pictures as a souvenir at the end of the party.

Make sure the pony gets water and rest at some point in the party.

People

You really should have as many as horses are running that year, usually eight to ten.

If you want to send invitations instead of calling, why not visit a local stable and get enough hay to include a bit in each envelope? Be sure to include a warning on the outside of the envelope: "Open Carefully."

Environment

For centerpieces, have bunches of fresh carrots with the greenery still attached. Visit a toy store for toy horseshoes. Tie them with a ribbon and give to guest to wear when they arrive. Also have signs around with phony quotes from past winners: *"I did this on carrots and hay...think what I could have done if I had a decent meal!" - Secretariat*. Call the library for lists of past winners.

Food

Food for this event can be elegant or picnic-y. Whatever you serve, Mint Juleps or Mint Tea are must. They are traditionally served at Churchill Downs along with strawberries and fresh cream.

Time

Make banners, get toy horseshoes, glass bowl for bets; prepare the Horseshoe Game. Get a pony and appropriate hats. Get a Polaroid camera and someone to take guests' pictures.

Special Notes for this Party

If you can't afford a pony for guests to sit on, use a sawhorse and attach ears and a tail. Cheaper and a lot funnier. Make a "saddle" out of a pillow strapped to the top with a belt.

Those folks who live in town with either their offsprings or parents on Mother's or Father's Day, usually do something traditional: dinner, brunch or a family excursion. One year, however, I was visiting in New York on the second Sunday in May and was invited to dinner at a friend's home where we played all sorts of "mother-themed" games. It occurred to me that whether you were with Mom, or a friend, that Mother's Day could be spruced up with some fun activities. This party is easily adapted to Father's Day.

Event

Mother's Day is celebrated on the second Sunday in May and Father's Day is observed on the second Sunday in June. We usually get together in the early afternoon, but you could certainly celebrate in the evening just as well. My friend created a funny game called *Name that Mother.* The game featured questions about famous women who are also mothers. Sample question: *"What famous film star (a mother) was driven to fits by wire coat hangers?"* (Answer: Joan Crawford). My friend passed out paper and pencils and quizzed the guests. She had questions about The Queen Mother (Elizabeth.) She had questions about "The Most Married Mother" (Elizabeth Taylor.) She had questions about every mother at the party. They were funny. They were serious. There were prizes. There was nostalgia. For your party, why not have everyone (men, too) come dressed as a famous mother? Mother Macree, Mommy Dearest, Mother Teresa, Lillian Carter, etc. For Father's Day, Father Time, Father of Our Country (George Washington) etc.

Play *Mother's Advice*: Have everyone make a list of ten important things to remember when bringing up children: *"Be sure to feed them," "Don't forget them at the grocery store," "Be nice to them, you may have to live with them someday."*

Award prizes for *Name That Mother* contest, funniest mother costume, most original mother, *Best Mother's Advice*, etc.

Give prizes every mother can use: blindfold, can of Campbell's chicken noodle soup, rope to tie up children, phony certificate for two week's vacation in the country.

Go to a second-hand bookstore for Dr. Spock's Baby and Child Care book, copy of Parent's Magazine, magazines with pictures of famous mothers and fathers.

People

Your family and/or friends. Not over twelve people unless they're all family members. You want to keep this party intimate. If the party is all friends with no "mom" present, crown someone "Mother" for the Day. It doesn't have to be a woman. This person will dispense advice, love, and band-aids throughout the party. Be sure to give "mom" a little purse full of band-aids, M&M's, Hershey Kisses, and little red hearts with which to tend to the offsprings.

Environment

Decorate with pictures of famous mothers/fathers and copies of Parent's Magazine. Feature pictures of your own mom and dad at all ages and in all situations. For music, make an extended tape of The Mamas and the Papas.

Food

Serve "there, there" food. That's the food your mom served when she said: *"There, there. Everything is going to be okay."* Things like fried chicken, chicken soup, steak, or roast beef with mashed potatoes, a green vegetable and salad. And even though my mom never made homemade ice cream for dessert topped with chocolate fudge and nuts, I think it's a great choice. Have slices of bananas, strawberries and pineapple available for toppings.

Time

Visit second hand book store for supplies, make up mother/father quiz. Plan, buy and prepare menu, shop for prizes.

Special Notes for this Party

If this is a family gathering and your mom/dad isn't present, this is perfect time to make a video of the whole family to send as a Mother's/Father's Day card.

Somehow everyone wants to have or go to a party on these two weekends marking the beginning and end of summer. It doesn't have to be a big deal - or it can be. In any case, have people over. It's a perfect outdoor nostalgic opportunity that will be remembered as one of the great parties if you give people a chance to have a real *Americana Holiday.*

Event

Memorial Day is the last Monday in May and is celebrated all weekend, so choose your day. Labor Day Weekend is the first weekend in September. These both really are *day* parties, perfect for hauling out all those old traditional outdoor party events: the three-legged race, the sack race, relay races, pig dressing contest, pie eating contests, and/or wheelbarrow races. Visit a local trophy shop for inexpensive trophies, medals, and first, second and third prize ribbons. If you want to have the trophies engraved, go early to accommodate this.

Pig Dressing

Pig Dressing is a team relay involving two Designated Pigs (really good sports). They present themselves on all fours to their relay teams (a team of two) who at "go" begin to "dress the pig." Over their own clothes, the pigs are dressed in jockey shorts, boxer shorts, and long pants or some other combination of clothes over clothes. The pig then runs to the other end of the room, undresses himself, then runs back and presents the clothes to the next dressers. This is a game that begs for people with an open-minded sense of humor.

People

At least eight. This is a party where you can accommodate a lot of people with not much effort, so invite as many as you want. Use small paper plates for invitations and give red bandannas for favors. Have them printed with party particulars: Memorial Day 1991, whatever. Tie them around the guests' necks when they arrive.

Environment

Decorate with lots of red, white, and blue. On Memorial Day it's a must to display the American Flag. In small towns there are parades that end with people visiting cemeteries to honor their war dead. It would be a nice thing and add some weight to the day to display pictures of family members who were involved in any war. On Labor Day, feature pictures of workers and encourage people to notice the real intent of the day. Make tapes of marching band music and pipe it out to the backyard. Make sure there is plenty of shade for people and provide sunblock and hats and plenty of water as well as softdrinks.

Food

People pretty much expect and hanker for good old Americana picnic food (hot dogs, hamburgers, watermelon, etc.). For those who don't eat red meat, make falafel burgers or serve turkey and chicken franks and/or grill fresh vegetables brushed with olive oil.

Time

Plan games, shop for trophies for awards, plan, buy and prepare food.

Special Notes for this Party

Ask guests to take turns telling about the most memorable Memorial Day/Labor Day they experienced as they were growing up.

Flag Day is such a neglected day that it's not even on my calendar. Not to worry, I actually remember when it is: June 14. This day marks the anniversary of the day in 1777 when Congress adopted the Stars and Stripes as the national emblem of the United States.

Event

Flag Making Contest and *Capture the Flag.* Have guests create their own flags during the party. Do it with paper if you insist, but it's a perfect time to use up all the scraps of fabric that were too swell to throw away and to small to use for anything else. Give prizes for prettiest, most significant, funniest, etc. For awards, look for things that feature stars and stripes or that are star shaped as well as miniature American, Confederate and regional flags.

Besides the event of making the flags, play one of my most favorite, rowdy games, *Capture the Flag.* This is not for the faint of heart, so choose guests carefully.

Capture the Flag

The play of the game goes like this: Each team has a flag (or handkerchief, but you will have just created these beautiful flags, so why not use one?) and each team wants to steal the flag of the other team.

Divide into the two teams. Make a circle at each end of the playing area. This marks the spot where the home flag lives and where you want to put your opponent's "captured" flag when you win the game. The hard part is not only stealing his flag, but making sure yours is still there when you bring your booty home. This can be a very rough game if you don't set down some ground rules. It's against the rules to put the flag in your pocket or under your clothes when you are defending or stealing.

When I played this game long ago, we played indoors in the gym. Protectors and thieves were designated (within one's own team, no need to tell the opposition) and the lights were turned out. In the gym, the flag had to be in the free throw circle on either side. You can imagine the mayhem in the dark. If you don't have an all-purpose, pretty empty room, outdoors seems like the best idea. But the dark was surely fun!

People

At least eight healthy specimens. This is going to be a physical day. Warn guests in advance that there will be some combat and to dress accordingly. If you want to send invitations, either include a tiny flag or create one from fabric and cover it with acetate and write party particulars across it.

Environment

For decorations, make some flags representing significant events in your life or the lives of your guests. Use patriotic music to put people in the mood of things: "God Bless America," "Hooray for the Red, White, and Blue," "I'm a Yankee Doodle Dandy," "It's a Grand Old Flag," etc.

Food

If you're in an area where a clam bake is feasible, that's a good idea. So is anything that lends itself to red, white and blue. There are many different chicken recipes that feature cherries. Add cherry cobbler and cherry pie with vanilla ice cream with blueberry topping and you'll have a patriotic-looking menu. For non-sugar eaters, use strawberry, blueberry and vanilla yogurt layered in champagne glasses. Lace with Grapenut sprinkles and layer with bananas.

Time

Assemble art supplies for contest, arrange game logistics, plan, buy and prepare food prizes, buy prizes, choose, buy and tape music.

Special Notes for this Party

To make the flags really look official, be sure to get a supply of dowels. Have a staple gun available so flags can be attached when they are finished.

► Fourth of July Party

I love the Fourth of July. One year, I was so out of control I actually made vests for all my guests. They were reversible with red and white stripes on one side and navy blue on the other. One of the guests who was here recently told me that even though it was twelve years ago, she still has the vest. It *was* fun.

Event

America's Birthday. Play ***Patriotic Charades and American Trivia***. Use titles like: "Glory," "Born on the Fourth of July," "Platoon," "Battle Hymn of the Republic," *"Give me liberty or give me death," "Ask not what our country can do for you, but what you can do for your country."* This is a time for patriotic songs, "down home" games, fireworks, home-made ice cream and watermelon. At my "vest-party", I asked all the guests to wear white if possible, to show off their vests.

One of the guests was lucky enough to have been born on the 4th of July, so every hour on the hour, we made a lot of noise and presented him with a silly present. My then-teenage daughters favored us with a funny tap dance routine and my old favorite standby game (Charades) did not desert me. I typed up all sorts of historical quotes (*"The British are coming!"* etc.) and put them in a glass jar. I also made up some gag sayings...supposedly said by famous people during their historical moment, e.g., Benjamin Franklin on discovering electricity: *"Shocking!"*

After dark we had a fireworks show around the pool. It wasn't elaborate, just skyrockets and sparklers. This is also a great day for sack, three-legged, and wheelbarrow races, etc.

Environment

Red, white, and blue everything. Streamers, balloons, and of course, flags all over the place. Tape patriotic music ("God Bless America," "Hooray for the Red White and Blue," "I'm a Yankee Doodle Dandy," "It's a Grand Old Flag," etc.).

Food

We served all the normal Fourth of July foods; wieners, hamburgers, watermelon, and the guests even helped make the ice cream. (Today, I would include an "American Grill" featuring grilled vegetables brushed with olive oil.)

Time

Make favors, buy legal fireworks, plan, buy and assemble food, cook-out supplies, tape patriotic songs.

Special Notes for this Party

Sometimes people forget all the details involved with this kind of party. Here's a reminder: supplies of charcoal, fire starters, matches, paper plates, napkins, ice chest or tub for drinks, ice for both tub and ice cream freezer, ice cream salt, ice cream freezer, wieners, hamburgers, watermelon, recipe for ice cream, sunscreen for guests, insect repellent, etc.

Some of the most innovative parties I have ever been to are given by an Emmy award-winning writer (Carl Sautter) and television producer (Paul Waigner). They *always* feature an event. And this is one of my favorites.

Event

Pumpkin Carving Party. A great party to be held anytime from the last week of October until Thanksgiving. Carl and Paul's guests gathered at 8 p.m., were handed a number designating their pumpkin, had a drink, and waited for all the guests to gather. Within about 15 minutes, we matched our numbers to numbers on the pumpkins. The hosts had gathered a variety of pumpkins in all shapes and sizes. Each had a number taped to it. Some pumpkins were smaller and so #5 might end up being three small pumpkins, and #7 might be a pumpkin with two small squash, but each guest got his own vegetable(s) to sculpt.

Since the partygoers included a lot of show business types, some of them professional artists, there were some really magnificent creations. There were enough guests on my own relatively kindergarten level that I did not feel too self-conscious, although I do admit I considered not signing my pumpkin!

After the carving and during the buffet dinner, everyone viewed all the creations. Each entry had been titled by the artist. All artists were invited to participate in judging. Prizes were given for prettiest, most humorous, most political, most environmental, scariest, etc.

Prize ideas include ribbons printed: Annual Pumpkin Carving Contest First place, Second place, etc., lottery tickets, and pumpkin seeds.

People

Although their party was quite large, this is a party which lends itself to any size crowd. Encourage guests to arrive on time. Tell them the starting gun will be fired 15 minutes after invited time. They will need to arrive on time to get their pumpkin, their place, and begin at the official "Carving Kickoff!" Ask guests to bring their own carving instruments. If you are not providing a favor apron, have them bring something to protect their clothes from the work.

Environment

Set up more working tables than you think you will need. That way people can spread out. If possible provide work areas housing 4 to 5 carvers as this will add to the feeling of fraternity. Stock your tables with crepe paper, pins, pipe cleaners, buttons, any odds and ends that seem as though they might have some creative possibilities. Also radishes, scallions and other vegetables could be worked into one's creation. If your tables are priceless antiques, cover them with blankets to protect them and put large slabs of plywood over that to use as carving surfaces. Cover the plywood with rolls of large butcher paper to insure an easy cleanup.

Food

For your buffet, how about a hearty stew? It's delicious, easy, and a great cold-weather food as well. Make it with meat or with sweet potatoes as the base. Another idea is pumpkin stuffed-ravioli. Just stew and flavor the pumpkin and fold into pasta dough. A green vegetable and salad with pumpkin pie for dessert completes the meal.

Time

Set up work tables with supplies; plan, buy and prepare food; get pumpkins and other veggies for carving; get paper towels, garbage bags, prizes.

Special Notes for this Party

To add a macabre note, call their answering machines and leave your message a la Vincent Price or any other ghoulish voice you prefer...maybe a few ghostly sounds. If they answer the phone, you'll probably just want to act like a normal person and issue a simple invitation.

Costume Party

The most traditional type of Halloween party is the Costume Party. An imaginative Los Angeles agent, J. Michael Bloom, gives an annual party that has people angling for invitations for months before the event.

Event

Halloween Costume Extravaganza. Held anytime during the week prior to Halloween, it gives guests an excuse to loosen up and live out a few fantasies. Since there are guests who might think getting a costume together is too much trouble, Michael provides a little incentive in the guise of some really spectacular prizes: television sets, 10-speed bikes, CD players. There's never a dull moment as he also has other activities going on before the Costume Parade. He hires two or three palm readers, tarot card readers, astrologers, etc., who are stationed in strategic places around the party. He also has a strolling magician or two. These are all things to keep the many strangers at the party involved and talking to one another.

Michael's party is very large; however, a much smaller, less expensive version would work just as well. You don't have to have expensive prizes. Dead hands (old gloves filled with kitty litter) would thrill (!) any recipient. Shrunken heads (balloons blown up half way up with faces drawn on them) and all variations on that theme are also well received.

If you can't afford a real magician (and you'd be surprised if you look in the yellow pages and offer someone $25 what you might come up with), enlist a friend to just do his "imitation" of a magician or go to the library, get out a magic book, learn a few tricks and do them yourself. Mind readers (phony or otherwise) are also a treat. The point is to have something for the guests to focus on. Halloween is such a great excuse for acting stupid. There's no point in missing the opportunity.

People

Have as many people as you like. My own optimum list is somewhere between eight and twelve.

Environment

If possible, hold this party in a haunted house. Lacking that, haunt your own. Party stores, esoteric book stores, and nature stores all sell tapes of thunderstorms and rain. Buy them and tape those together with some wicked laughter and moans and play it all evening. Believe me, your friends will buy it. Tell guests a long story about the "strange goings on" that have always occurred in your house, but you've never told them 'til now. They'll know you are putting them on...probably...but it will still be eerie. Use candles and flashlights inside pumpkins to make them come alive! When guests arrive, be sure to take a picture of them in their costumes immediately.

If you really want to scare your guests to death, enlist the help of a cohort to be "dead" for the evening. Rig some kind of casket for them to lay in. Arrange a "viewing" area. Encourage them to lie perfectly still until "viewers" are peering for a close look and then either open one eye, sit up quickly and lay back down, or moan.

Food

Have a cold weather dish like pot roast, apple pie or cobbler and apple cider. Carry the theme further and bob for apples! One of my favorite pasta recipes combines steamed sliced zucchini, slivered almonds, scallions, garlic and olive oil and would be a great alternative for non-meat eaters. Stew apples with lemon juice, cinnamon and raisins and serve on a crisp flour tortilla for a sugarless dessert. Top with sour cream.

Time

Arrange for palm readers, tarot card readers, astrologers, magicians, make prizes, plan, buy and prepare food, arrange for your own costume.

Special Notes for this Party

There are people who are put off by even funny things having to do with the occult, so make sure those on your guest list will approve.

► Dia de Los Muertos Party (Day of the Dead)

More and more Anglos are beginning to celebrate the Mexican equivalent of Halloween which is called Dia de Los Muertos.

Event

Dia de Los Muertos. In Mexico, The Day of the Dead, celebrated from October 30 to November 2, is a happy occasion where families have picnics at cemeteries to visit their dead friends and relatives. They take favorite foods of the deceased, dress up as skeletons and actually talk to the dead.

It's a big event celebrated with sugar skulls and sugar bread called "Pan Muertos" (dead bread). There are skeletons playing guitars, dog skeletons, dentist skeletons, etc.

I like the idea of having a party with all my dead friends but if this somehow doesn't appeal to you, why not your own version of Day of the Dead? Feature a *Dead Celebrities Contest, a Talk to the Dead* interlude, and for your more cerebral guests, advertise a lecture on *"The Joys of Being Dead"*. I'm sure there will be a real glut of Elvis Presleys all arguing that they aren't dead anyway. The lecture can include the many advantages the dead have over the living: no dental problems, no weight problems, no high rent, no need for face lift, etc., etc.

A Ouija Board is perfect for contacting the dead. Your local toy store has a selection of ghost-oriented games you can buy. There are all sorts of possibilities.

Give bones for favors. Magic shops are a source for all kinds of "dead" ideas. For prizes, shrunken heads (decorated balloons barely blown up) will delight all (but psychologists) and dead hands (gloves filled with kitty litter or flour) add a creepy touch.

87

People

Best is eight or more. It doesn't take a lot of people, just lots of ideas!

Environment

Visit second-hand bookshops for old magazines featuring pictures of dead celebrities for decorations. Drape them in black ribbons and black crepe paper. Have macabre music playing as guests arrive. Have hands of the dead and shrunken heads hanging about in startling places. Use music from requiem mass and a funeral dirge for atmosphere.

Food

Cajun food appeals to me for this party. Jambalaya, gumbo, red beans, rice, cole slaw, corn bread or any Paul Prudhomme recipes will enhance the atmosphere. For dessert, sweet potato pie. Don't forget the sugar skulls and other macabre goodies available. Be sure to serve Pan Muertos. Feature favorite foods of the dead e.g., Elvis peanut butter and banana sandwiches, etc.

Time

Improvise your own Pan Muertos and sugar figures if there is no Mexican bakery around; collect pictures for decorations; plan, buy and prepare food, make prizes, get bones.

Special Notes for this Party

Again, be sure your guests are not put off by Ouija boards and the like.

► Political Parties (no pun intended)

Lots of people like to celebrate election night. They gather in front of the television set and watch the returns come in. Some years it's boringly one-sided. Other years, it's close and filled with tension. Whatever the case, it's not only an interesting night for a party, it may end up inspiring some guests to get with it and vote before they arrive.

Event

Voters' Lament Party. The first Tuesday after the first Monday in November marks Election Day. Although the television will be the center of attention throughout the evening, there will be those long blocks of time when nothing appears to be happening. Use those times for a **Political Trivia Quiz** gleaned from promises of the current candidates. It will be interesting to know how aware people are of who promised what. For prizes, get rubber masks of Nixon, Kennedy, and other former presidents.

At your next break from viewing, *"Pin the Tail on the Donkey" and "Pin the Trunk on the Elephant* will help the group not take things so seriously.

People

Any number. Visit a toy store and get miniature elephants and donkeys. String them on red, white and blue ribbons and put them over your guest's necks as they arrive. Be careful! Make sure you give the right symbol to the right guest. Have Bull Mooses (remember Teddy Roosevelt) available for those in neither major party.

Environment

Decorate in traditional colors and feature pictures of the current candidates. If you have several television sets, spot them all over the house so that guests can wander about.

Feature political ("Happy Days Are Here Again," "Camelot") and patriotic ("It's a Grand Old Flag," "The Star Spangled Banner") music.

Food

Politicians always complain about the "creamed chicken circuit" when they are on the campaign trail, so by all means, serve creamed chicken and peas. Add corn bread, cole slaw and apple pie for dessert. Another "campaign circuit" favorite is chicken pot pie. Make it without chicken for vegetarians. For sugarless dessert, make baked apples with butter, raisins, pecans and cinnamon.

How about serving conservative portions to the Republicans and you-know-what to the opposition? It might be the one time Republicans will think of defecting. If not now, when?

Time

Make up trivia quiz; find pictures for decorations; make "Pin the Tail/Trunk" game; get straight pins; plan, buy and prepare food; set up viewing areas.

Special Notes for this Party

This party could be an opportunity to encourage people to vote. Invite people to come straight from the polling booths. Be sure to discuss how important it is to be one of the people who "make a difference" when you issue the invitation. Mention there will be a special "treat" for those who arrive with balloting stubs, then give them all "good citizenship medals," you make out of felt and gold cord or improvise a special cookie.

On Thanksgiving, there's usually so much going on with the cooking that having any goal other than filling the stomachs rarely occurs to us. In fact, there are a few simple ideas that can add other dimensions to the day.

Event

Thanksgiving is usually celebrated the fourth Thursday of November, but, our family has been known to celebrate the Sunday before or after depending on which members of our family are in or out of town. The day isn't the important part, it's all about being together. At our home it's traditional for everyone to make some part of the meal. Instead of bringing the dish already prepared, the fun is that we do it together in my kitchen.

I'm usually responsible for the turkey and I begin preparations the night before. First thing in the morning, I put it in the oven and start assembling the stuffing. My daughter Kelly is the pumpkin pie baker and she usually arrives first to get the pie in the oven. I love having her there next to me rolling and sifting. I can pretend for a minute that the kids still all live at home!

Close friends and family members are usually watching one of a series of ball games or making one of the 700 trips to the grocery store for items I forgot. It would spoil the tradition if I made a list.

Before or after the meal, we all join hands around the table and take turns listing those things we are most grateful for in the past year. This is one of those traditions for which my children used to roll their eyes heavenward, but it is now one of their favorites.

I guess we all have memories of Thanksgiving and Christmas dinners with many generations all gathered together with card tables set up all over the house. The adults at the big table with children all seated together off in some corner. I fondly remember graduating from the little table to the big table and finally seating my children at the little tables. Today, my children are at the big table and it won't be too long before card tables will appear for their children. There's a certain continuity of life represented at these ritual gatherings... I wouldn't miss one.

Another nice thing to do on Thanksgiving (which I mentioned in Chapter 1) is to ask each guest to add something to his clothing right before dinner, to help recreate the feel of the original Thanksgiving dinner.

My friend, Jean, has a great Thanksgiving tradition at her house. They call it *The Gobbler Contest.* Years ago, they converted an old cone-shaped "witch" hat into a turkey comb by adding red crepe paper down one side. Every year, it's passed around the table. When the hat gets to you, you "Gobble." The "best gobbler" doesn't have to do any dishes.

People

Any number of real or extended family. Be sure everyone gets his cooking assignment in plenty of time. My preference is for people to all cook together in my kitchen and I have the space to accommodate that. It doesn't matter how you do it, just have a good time.

Environment

Decorate as little or as much as you have time for. I don't decorate a lot for this holiday as I feel the aroma of a turkey wafting through the house automatically sets the spirit on "Turkey Day." Create placecards that are "reproductions" of the first Thanksgiving placecards: written on either dried corn husks or any whole vegetable like small sweet potatoes or russets. It's also a nice touch to have a big pumpkin situated either by the front door or on the table. Have black markers and ask guests to write on the pumpkin what they are most thankful for and to sign it. Then use the pumpkin as the centerpiece of not only the table but conversation. Be sure to have a camera ready to record the gathering. If you have a camcorder, catch various portions of the day...as each guest arrives, presents his dish, talks about Thanksgiving and takes his leave.

Food

I'm a stickler for tradition on this day and serve turkey, dressing, sweet potatoes, cranberry sauce, salad, bread, green vegetable and pumpkin pie. These days, more and more people are forgoing not only red meat and poultry, but any product that is animal related. For those folk, there are many tofu recipes to replace turkey as the main course. If tofu doesn't appeal to you, just make sure there are lots of vegetables. Serve them with ceremony.

Time

Provide for viewing area; set up extra tables and chairs; get camera and film; plan, shop and prepare food; assign dishes as well as cooking time to cooks; plan costume for dinner.

Special Notes for this Party

As with all parties, but particularly this one, the main point is for all to have an easy, relaxed time. If a dish doesn't turn out right or someone is late, the attitude is always, "It's okay. We're all together. That's what matters." And in fact, that is true. At the end of the meal, when everyone is stuffed and thinks they will never eat again, have a group walk. Not only is it good for you, it shakes down the meal and makes room for the pumpkin pie when you return. Be sure to take the camera.

► Christmas Parties

There are so many wonderful excuses for get-togethers at Christmastime. One of my favorites helps me get into the Christmas Spirit and begin Christmas Shopping at the same time.

Event

Christmas Swap Meet. Last year I was invited to a wonderfully chaotic party where people swapped their best Christmas baking efforts ("I'll give you a dozen Snicker-doodles for one Yule Log"), unloaded a year's accumulation of unwanted presents, made new friends and had a great party all at the same time.

All presents are tagged with the owner's name. Someone picks up something, holds it in the air, says, "Who's does this belong to? I want it." and the Christmas Swap begins.

People

Whatever works. At least eight. If you are smart, you'll invite all the best cooks you know. The best time to hold this party is the first Saturday morning in December. As guests arrive, have them arrange their baked goods and their unwanted presents on tables labeled: *"Goodies"* or *"I don't want it, you might."*

No fair starting until everyone is present. Be stringent about a starting time. Even the beginning of December is a busy time so if you plan it for 10 a.m., tell them swapping will start at precisely 10:15 and stick to it.

Environment

Make sure there are plenty of shopping bags for people to carry off their loot. Also pencils and paper for exchanging recipes and phone numbers. Play Christmas music. Put everyone in a good mood by answering the door in a Santa Claus hat, whiskers, and red sweat clothes.

Food

Serve coffee, juice, fruit, danish, conversation and spirited trading!

Time

Produce your best goodie, gather unwanted gifts, label them.

Special Notes for this Party

Don't take time for lots of preparation for this party. Call people in the middle of November and alert them so they can begin thinking about it and gathering swap items. Follow-up a few days before the party to remind people. Two hours is plenty of time during this busy time of the year. Stress in the invitations that the event will be held from 10 to 12 and then it is *over*. More people will come that way and you will feel more like having it.

Tree Trimming

Okay, I know I've said it before, but really this *is* my favorite party. Not only is it one of my favorite times of the year anyway, but when I gave this party originally, it was the first time I ever had a party and did anything other than saying: *"Come for dinner, or dessert, or to play cards."*

Event

Tree Trimming Party. The best part of this party is that each guest has to make an ornament for the tree made of something in his home at the time the invitation was extended. Even people who are not adept with their hands find a way to make something interesting if they put their minds to it. Stress they must only use those things they already have in their home. This not only is a creative challenge, it keeps people from going completely crazy in their creative endeavors.

When guests arrive, have them "hide" their ornament until *The Ornament Saga.* I put the lights on the tree ahead of time so that once dinner is finished, we are all ready to begin decorating the tree.

Since it is such a busy evening, I serve dinner right away as we are all anxious to begin. After dessert, I gather everyone around the tree. It's now "time." Guests retrieve their ornament and get ready to show their creation. As part of presenting it to the group, the artists tell what a struggle it was to make, and how they came up with their inspiration. The guest then puts the ornament on the tree. Each guest takes his turn until the tree is finished. Since I love to give prizes so much, I make up categories to fit the creations: "prettiest," "most political," "gaudiest," "tiniest," etc.

You can play a Christmas version of Charades, too, if you want to. A few years ago, I was in Alaska at Christmastime appearing in a play, so my Christmas Party was with my "theater family." We were performing the play

"Steel Magnolias," so I got everyone to sit still for a game of *Steel Magnolias Charades*.

I had already typed up lines from the play and put them on little strips of paper. Instead of choosing teams, we just went through the group for two or three rounds. Each of us got up, pantomimed the name of the character whose speech it was and then acted out the speech.

Even though we were familiar with the lines, it was fun to see how hard it was for everyone to remember them in this context. We loved getting to act so silly.

Make up your own custom tailored *Christmas Charades* out of your own guests' experiences or use Christmas titles: "I'm Dreaming of a White Christmas," "A Charlie Brown Christmas," "All I Want for Christmas Is My Two Front Teeth," "The Gift of the Magi," "The Long Christmas Dinner," etc.

· The night wouldn't be complete for me without singing Christmas Carols. Although most people know words to these familiar songs, it's nice to provide song sheets. I always conclude the carols with "White Christmas" and "Silent Night" right after I have done my favorite: *"K's 12 Days of Christmas."* Instead of using the lyrics everyone is familiar with, have each guest make up a word or line. The leader starts singing with *"On the first day of Christmas, my true love sent to me, a ..... in a pear tree."* You might say a Jaguar, a chocolate bar, a day off, or whatever you covet. As the singing continues and you get to *"the second day,"* the leader then points to the next guest who takes *"The second day of Christmas my true love sent to me ... two days off...and a ...JAGUAR (or whatever the first person said) in a pear tree.* The song continues. If you have less than 12 people," just start over again with the next person in line until the song is over. It's necessary to have a someone with a loud voice (and who knows the song) who will keep it going. It may or may not end up being melodic, but it always ends up being fun.

Every year when I get out my ornaments, I think of all the friends who made them and the stories that accompanied them. One of my favorites is a little prescription bottle with a ribbon hanger on it. The label reads: *"Rx for happiness."* Inside were little pieces of paper that read "laughter," "good friends," "singing," etc. Each year I sprinkle the words on my tree and each year, when I take the tree down, I retrieve the papers and think of the friend who created it.

I admit that after cooking, getting the house ready, etc., I usually am dashing around at the eleventh hour throwing an ornament together. Not being particularly blessed with drawing skills, I find I have just enough talent to represent the simple shape of trees with cinnamon sticks, toothpicks, keys, etc. I also have an interesting array of ornaments made from castoff Dr. Pepper cans (from those years when I was so addicted). Tin snips are a wondrous thing.

People

Any number. When you issue the invitation, stress the ornament-making part of the party. Let them know the rules about making it. Tell them that it doesn't have to be beautiful or fabulous, it just has to be home-made and that there will be prizes. Tell them to bring it in some concealed way, as there will be an official moment in the evening when the ornaments are presented and talked about. Again, be specific about arrival time as there are many events during this evening. I usually make a favor the guest can wear. Sometimes, I just make wreath-necklaces by cutting up long strings of gold or silver tinsel. One year I took wide red ribbon about a yard long and sewed on jingle bells and draped them around each guest's neck like scarves.

Environment

I like to trim the house with ornaments from previous parties with the creator's name prominently displayed along with greens, ribbons, and candles and babies breath. I use only the lights of the tree, candles and the fireplace for illumination for this party.

It's not necessary to be elaborate, just make sure it's festive. A good way to do that is to give the guests something to wear (a tinsel garland, whatever). It loosens people up and makes them more participatory. A party hat with mistletoe is loaded with possibilities. A byproduct of this party is all the wonderful memories.

Food

I like to serve hot apple cider with cinnamon sticks for stirrers to people as they come in the door on a cold winter night. Although I also serve wine, most people end up sticking with the cider. I have a big pantry of hard liquor available, but find that given other interesting beverages, people are opting more and more for wine, spritzers, sparkling water and, in this case, cider.

Serve whatever you like for dinner. Steaming mugs of chowder or vegetable soup are comforting cold weather starters. The Scandinavian Christmas ritual is oyster stew. Turkey and dressing are of course, traditional, and I find them easy to prepare for a big group. Split baked sweet potatoes in half and serve with a dollop of sour cream sprinkled with cinnamon. This is a healthier and simpler alternative to traditional holiday sweet potatoes doctored mercilessly with brown sugar, marshmallows, butter, pecans, etc., and it's every bit as delicious.

Cranberry sauce, a salad and broccoli end up balancing off the main course, with pumpkin pie for dessert. Serve stewed pears with cinnamon and butter as an alternative for sugarless guests.

Time

Buy tree, string lights on it, make favors; plan, gather and prepare food; get prizes, Christmas Carol books, mistletoe; make up charades material.

Special Notes for this Party

More and more people are choosing to share their Christmas experiences with strangers. A children's ward at a hospital would get a big lift out of a party featuring homemade decorations and a madeup "12 Days of Christmas" rendition.

99

▶ New Year's Eve Party

Because New Year's Eve has gotten such a bad rap for drinking and outrageous behavior, many people don't venture out of the house on that night. Others don't gather on New Year's Eve because they don't have anyone to kiss at midnight or don't want to kiss the person they have! My solution deals with all of the above and it's (I know, I keep saying this!) one of my favorite parties.

Event

New Year's Eve Past and Present. On New Year's Eve, I have a party that begins at 6 p.m. and ends at 8 p.m. I make it clear the party is not "drop-in" and that guests will be able to go on to other parties if they like or be home before the streets become too dangerous.

I invite a psychic to advise us concerning the coming year. So far, I've been able to find a psychic through referrals of friends. If you don't have that option, check the yellow pages for Occult Shops as a resource. I usually end up paying $75 for two hours. I put a table with a candle and timer in a bedroom and guests go in privately. They each usually spend about 5 minutes a piece. I tell the psychic ahead of time so he knows how much time to allot per person to make sure everyone is accommodated. Guests line up and go in on their own.

Because it was the end of a decade in 1989, I got a great idea which I have since added to my annual ritual. When guests arrived, I pointed to a stack of index cards and pencils with a sign that said:

"Please note the best thing that happened to you in the 80's and the worst thing that happened to you. Be prepared to read this at 8 p.m. Prizes will be awarded."

The reason I told folks when they came in the door was to allow them to think about it during the evening. This is a subject that, given a few moments, brings up many possibilities. For prizes I gave a date book for best thing that happened and a set of screw drivers (which seemed appropriate) for the person who had the worst thing happen to him.

While they were thinking, I attached a sign to each guest's back for a *Who Am I?* game. I used newsmakers of the '80s and included everyone from Klaus Von Bulow to Gary Hart. It was hilarious.

Since it will be ten years before you can ask the "decade" question, just ask for the past year. I also give favors of black-eyed peas (twelve peas - one for each month) tied in white tulle with tiny red ribbons. An old Southern custom says that if you sleep with black-eyed peas under your pillow on New Year's Eve, you will have money for the rest of the year. Explain this to your guests as you tell them goodnight and press one into their hand.

Environment

I'm always looking for an excuse to dress up and invite my friends to do the same if they are so inclined. There are so few occasions when we get a chance to dress up, it's a shame to miss one. This way we not only look elegant but it makes us feel as though we are getting the New Year off to a "Grand Start."

The evening is quite simple. Candlelight only. Everyone eats and compares notes on what the psychic said or what they're going to ask. Either play beautiful classical violin music or big band music a la Guy Lombardo.

People

Less than twenty. Too many people at this party spoils the intimacy. Also you want to be able to get everyone into see the psychic in the two hours you have. As usual, be specific. This year a guest who comes every year to my party didn't arrive until 7 p.m. and was all upset. I had not told him to *be on time* because I thought he would remember. People are so in the habit of getting "drop in" invitations for New Year's Eve (and other occasions) that you must *say:*
"This is not a drop in party. Because this is New Year's Eve and many people either do not want to be on the road late or are going on to other parties, this

*party will start promptly at 6 p.m. and will end promptly at 8 p.m. Food will be
served, but this is not dinner."*

Food

Naturally one wants to serve champagne for New Year's Eve. For non-drinkers, I
serve freshly-squeezed orange juice in sparkling champagne glasses. It's every bit
as festive. Serve it from a beautiful glass pitcher and it's pretty hard to resist.

I put a ham on the table with a few slices already cut and a very sharp
knife, a tray with a selection of interesting mustards, baby croissants presliced in a
lovely glass cookie jar, and an eggplant/vegetable concoction with pita bread for
my vegan friends.

Time

Hire a psychic; collect, cook and arrange the food; get candles and matches; buy
champagne; buy or make freshly-squeezed orange juice; arrange for champagne
glasses, and prepare good luck black-eyed peas. Dress up!

Special Notes for this Party

This is one night on which every effort should be made to provide guests with an
elegant and memorable experience. Be sure to give yourself time to rest and get
ready before people arrive.

Annual Parties

3   Annual Parties

This chapter includes parties geared toward other than "traditional" themes, "made up" holidays and some familiar ideas with a new twist.

▶   National Crayola Day Party

National Crayola Day grew out of a grade school reunion party weekend. As we all sat around and talked about the kids and teachers who endeared themselves to us, we talked about how much we loved coloring in our coloring books and eating peanut butter 'n' jelly sandwiches. Since we didn't figure to have a reunion every year and we did want to color, we decided to celebrate Dan Crayola.

Event

National Crayola Day. An important little-known holiday occurs in late April "marking" the day Dan Crayola invented his famous coloring device, ultimately named in his honor — The Crayon. As soon as each guest arrives, pin his name card on him with a big safety pin. Mark one of the signs with an unobtrusive symbol on the back. At the end of the party, when you are giving prizes for Best Coloring, Best Picture, Most Well Behaved, etc., the person with the symbol on the back will get a prize too.

Give each guest his own brand new box of crayons as soon as he arrives. Get the most expensive boxes you can afford. There is nothing more fun than looking at all those sharp, color graded crayons that have never been touched.

Have a stack of paper or buy several coloring books and tear the pages into piles. As the guests come in, put them to work choosing the pages they will color later. Decide immediately how many each person can color. If the guests color more than one, invite them to choose their best and enter into competition for prizes. Give adult coloring books for prizes or gold stars. Get regular coloring books or buy the new adult coloring books and use the crayon magic markers. Mainly, the most important thing is to have a wonderful variety of colors. Make comfortable work spaces for people. Ask the artists to sign their creations prior to the "Formal Showing," which can take place wherever you have enough room to display them (perhaps the dining room). Give awards for most beautiful, silliest, most color, least color, etc.

People

Any number, anytime. Saturday late morning is best. If you are into invitations, now's your chance. Pull out the construction paper, the triple box of Crayons and go to it. Make kindergarten-style drawings inviting your friends. Tell them you're celebrating the auspicious event by returning to kindergarten. Invite them to dress accordingly.

Environment

Decorate with counterfeit children's art work or enlist help for the real thing.

Food

Serve Kool Aid, peanut butter and jelly sandwiches, milk/chocolate milk, and graham crackers. I think all these foods sound cute and funny and I'd like to have a taste, but, if this party is at dinnertime, have some grown-up childhood food as a backup. Suggestions include fried chicken, mashed potatoes, green salad, spinach, and chocolate pie for dessert.

Time

Get coloring books, crayons, name tags, adult coloring books, gold stars, plan, buy and prepare food.

Special Notes for this Party

You don't have to go to a lot of trouble for this party. You can just have people over for dinner and break out the crayons.

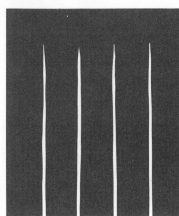

Haven't you ever watched the Olympics or the Celebrities "Battle of the Network Stars" on television and thought, "I can do that!" This is your chance to give you and your friends a shot at immortality or at least Andy Worhol's "Fifteen Minutes of Fame."

Event

The "Smith" Games. Name this day after yourself. Use your own name or the name of your suburb. Although this sounds like a game for a large group (and it can be) it's every bit as much fun with eight. When I first gave this party, I made "pennies" for everyone. A high school alternative to "shirts" and "skins" that resembles a sandwich board, but is made of cloth. A rectangular piece of cotton (denim, canvas, whatever) about 36" long, about twelve inches wide, with a hole cut out in the middle for the head and ties at each end (at the waist) to hold them on. I made four yellow "pennies" trimmed in blue and four blue ones trimmed in yellow. An easier solution is tying different colored ribbons around the arms of the participants to denote teams.

This year at my ***"Memorial Day Games,"*** I made fringed collars out of crepe paper for the each team. It's very simple: take a package of crepe paper, unwrap it, and do not unfold it. Cut across the paper at eight inch intervals. Next, cut these sections into fringe by cutting from botton to top, six inches (that leaves two inches for a border). Then, unfold the paper and cut this long piece of fringe into 15"-17" sections. You can either use scotch tape for closers or go to the fabric store and buy press on velcro dots for closers. I made 12 in about 5 minutes. They were darling and I was ecstatic to find something that I could make so quickly and looked so great. If you are feeling rich, have t-shirts printed as favors in two different colors and use them for game playing.

I still like to surprise my guests with the activities but I do say things like, ***"We'll be playing games outside so dress accordingly. Be sure to wear tennis shoes."*** As the guests arrived, the first order of the day was donning colors and finding out their teams.

It's important to put the teams together yourself. No one wants to be chosen last, and random assignments might produce an all-jock team with no competition.

I had a ping pong table, so there was a table tennis tournament with a bracket that diagramed who played who and when. You can make your own bracket or get one at a sporting goods store, usually for free.

There were the individual events (table tennis, darts) and the team events (badminton, three-legged races, wheelbarrow races, sack races).

Solo events counted points for "Best All-Round Sports Participant" and also added to team points. Same for couple events.

Obviously, very important to the success of a day like this is to keep it on schedule. Decide ahead of time when various events are to begin and end and stick to it.

We started with the races, moved to the front yard for badminton (blues against the yellows/best two out of three), went to the back yard for food and simultaneous table tennis and dart competition. There were both singles and doubles in the Ping Pong tournament.

The day ended with the presentation of trophies and ribbons. The first place team members all got blue ribbons and the second place team all got red ribbons. There were trophies for the Table Tennis Champion, for Ms./Mr. Congeniality and Ms./Mr. Spirit. Make sure there is a prize for everyone. I got trophies and ribbons at a local trophy shop. They didn't cost all that much and were worth their fun-weight in gold.

If you'd rather make the prizes yourself, here's an easy idea. Craft shops sell little wooden numbers and letters. Buy wooden "1s" and "2s" and screw tiny eye-screws into the tops. Then paint them white and string them on ribbons and present them to all the team members at the awards ceremony.

The three-legged race involves two participants each with one leg tied to the other. The wheelbarrow race is run with one person as the wheelbarrow and another driving the wheelbarrow. The wheelbarrow puts his hands on the ground, the driver takes that person's legs in his hands and together they run to the finish line. All these races can be run relay style.

People

At least eight. For hard copy enthusiasts, stop by a Western Union store and get some blanks and compose something like this:

"Bill Johnson. You have been selected to represent Singing Hills (your suburb) in the first annual "Smith Games." Please gather no later than 10 a.m. prepared for combat at Smith Field, address. Areas of testing will be table tennis, badminton, wheelbarrow races, (include all the events you are planning). The games will begin after weighing in (no one under 25 pounds may compete) and chemical testing (you will have to drink from a variety of fresh juices before competition to determine if your taste buds are in working order). The games will continue till sundown (or whenever) with closing ceremonies and awards at 7 pm. A victory celebration will follow. Please RSVP by xxx. A limited number of participants are invited. 213-555-5555."

Sign it: "The Smith Gaming Committee" or somesuch. As usual, follow-up with a phone call a couple of days later.

Environment

Since all the events take place outside, this event is best held in summer or late spring. Decorate with colored streamers. Choose the "Smith Colors" for decoration and make sure they match the "pennies", t-shirts or ribbons you have denoting team allegiance. Play "Call to the Post" (the music they play to begin horse races). "Call to the Post" is unavailable at music stores since it is not something one gets requests for often. Because it's only a few bars and it's in the public domain, I'm reproducing it for you right here.

Visit your local high school to find a student of the horn who would be happy to play into your tape recorder. Play this as a prelude to your races. Then play "Chariots of Fire" during the races. It's possible, of course, that you could pursuade your horn player to hang around all day playing "Call to the Post" at appropriate times for a few dollars. The horn playing will certainly add ambience if he'll stay - otherwise, pay him to tape it for you.

Food

Since the party is outside, have all outdoor food: hamburgers and hot dogs. Egg salad for vegetarians and vegetable salad for vegans. These salads taste great in hamburger and hot dog buns. We even made homemade ice cream in the electric ice cream mixer. It's no trouble that way and it adds an old-fashioned flavor to the festivities to hear it grinding away during the party. And it tastes even better than Dove Bars.

Time

Get game supplies, ribbons and trophies; plan, collect and prepare food; schedule games; procure and fill out brackets; get "Call to the Post" and "Chariots of Fire."

Special Notes for this Party

Make this party memorable for everyone by including enough areas for excellence that everyone takes home something. Give prizes for things like "Looks Best in Yellow," "Best Laugher," "Most Team Spirit," etc.

▶ National Tap Dance Day Party

Is there anyone who wouldn't like to know how to tap dance? There might be some people who wouldn't like this party, although I can't think of who that might be. If you can, don't invite them.

Event

National Tap Dance Day. Held anytime you want to have a fun party or on Ann Miller's birthday which is April 12. Transform everyone's secret fantasy into reality. It's not really that hard. I just called a local dance studio and asked to speak to someone who taught beginning tap dancing. I explained that I was having eight non-dancing guests to a party and that we wanted her to come for two hours and teach us a simple routine that we'd be able to put together at the end of the party for a recital.

It doesn't cost that much for two hours of a dance teacher's time. The woman brought a record, dutifully taught us all and presented us in our own version of "A Chorus Line" at the end of the evening. Although there were lots of eyes rolling back in the head at the beginning of the evening at the thought of this preposterous event, even the most skeptical guest managed to learn the routine and have a great time.

Give prizes for all participants. Announce categories that will enhance the party: Most Game, Best Dancer, Most Motivated Dancer, etc. Reward them with foot-related items: ankle bracelets, socks, toenail polish; or a foot of anything - stickers, licorice, beautiful ribbon, etc. For favors, give polaroids of the recital group and a tape of the music.

People

Any number. You don't need a huge amount of room if you don't invite a huge amount of people. I had eight people at my tap dancing party and it was a perfect number. Advise your guests to wear comfortable shoes, but preferably not tennis shoes.

Environment

When I gave this party in New York, it was in my carpeted living room, so I got several sheets of plywood (I borrowed them from a theater) and laid them side by side to dance on. It worked great.

Tap dancing is a great excuse to decorate with posters from old tap dance movies featuring Busby Berkley, Fred and Ginger, Shirley Temple, etc. Theater book stores are a great resource for supplies. Play Fred Astaire records as inspirational music when guests arrive.

Another option is to call this "A Chorus Line" and get cardboard top hats for the guests. My favorite is calling it *National Tap Dance Day* and using everything!

Food

Serve something light since you will be exercising. Pasta main dishes are a good idea. Toss it with garlic, olive oil, fresh basil and tomatoes. Pair it a with Caesar salad, steamed asparagus, garlic bread and fresh fruit for dessert.

Time

Arrange a hard surface to tap on, hire tap dance teacher, coordinate music, plan, collect and prepare food, buy prizes, arrange for favors.

Special Notes for this Party

Be prepared for responses of *"My God, what has she done this time,"* followed by *"When can we do this again?"* at the end of the party.

► Square Dance Party

When I was in high school, the nuns and priests instigated monthly square dances in their efforts to combat the evils of "rock 'n roll." While it didn't exactly stamp out Elvis Presley, it really was a lot of fun. And it still is. If you've got the space to pull this party together, your guests will beg you to have it annually.

Event

Square Dance Party. This party is not as big a deal as you might think. If you check the Yellow Pages in your town, you will undoubtedly find (through a dance studio) a referral to someone who teaches square dancing. Callers usually arrive with music and are complete unto themselves. They teach the steps and call the dances. Talk to them about your existing sound system. Frequently they bring their own amplifying apparatus.

If you want to have a theme to the party, call it an *"Oklahoma"* party and invite everyone to come as cowboys or farmers. Serve down-home food and play down-home games.

Pig Dressing Contest

Two teams line up. There are two Designated Pigs (poor humiliated people). They present themselves on all fours to the relay teams. Two people from each team have to dress the pig, the pig has to run to the other end of the room and back, undress and present the clothes to the next team. Over their own clothes, the pigs are dressed in any combination of clothes you can come up with: jockey shorts, boxer shorts, and long pants by their cowboys and farmers. Give prizes to all the cowboys and farmers on the team. A great idea is to have calico kerchiefs with the name and date of the party printed on them.

This party would be just as much fun with eight or eighty-eight. An elaborate version might take place at a local ranch and feature hay rides as part of the evening. This party is a terrific idea for a regularly scheduled party if you have the group to do it with.

People

Although, as I said in the beginning of the book, I like to invite all my friends to a Square Dance Party, this is a fun party for as small a number as eight. The key word here is eight. Either eight or multiples of eight. Make sure people know they don't have to come as couples, but that you do need an accurate count in order to make sure everyone has partners. If you have more men than women, provide a few funny wigs for men to wear who are playing women and if the problem is the opposite, provide hats for the women who will be playing men. Tell people ahead of time so they can dress for square dancing. If you are going to use "Oklahoma" as a theme, photocopy a large outline of the state, cover it with acetate and write party particulars across the face of that.

Environment

Stage this party on your backyard patio, in your garage or a hired hall. Decorate with bails of hay, pitchforks, old milk pails, cowboy hats, checkered table cloths and serve as many things as possible from baskets lined with checkered fabric or calico. Play the music from "Oklahoma" when you're not dancing. People will get very *hot,* so make sure you have lots of water and hand towels around.

Food

This party gives you a chance to grill steaks, ribs, chicken, corn on the cob, shish kebab of veggies and/or meat. Serve deep dish pie with ice cream for dessert.

Time

Hire teacher/caller; arrange for music/sound system; plan, collect and prepare food; get clothes for Pig Dressing; have bandannas printed.

Special Notes for this Party

If people are interested in sharing the responsibility, turn this party into a monthly or bi-monthly event.

► National Foot Day Party

Most chiropodists (foot doctors) don't even know about this day. I'm sure as soon as they hear about it, they will want to declare it a national holiday! It's a fun, silly evening or day.

Event

Foot Painting Party. This little-known holiday occurs whenever you decide you want a fun party. Although I gave this party in my New York apartment and didn't think a thing about it, you might be more inclined to feature this party during the summer when the main event can be staged outside. It might be wise to advise guests to dress in old clothes.

The highlight of the party is the *Foot Painting Contest.* Get two large cookie sheets and fill them with water based paint (so it will wash off easily). When I did it, I put hot pink in one, and brilliant yellow in the other. Your first thought might be that we are going to paint everyone's feet. Nope, at this party, the guests will paint *with* their feet.

I went to the butcher shop and bought a huge roll of paper for the artists to paint on. With one person on each side to steady him (that paint gets slick!), he steps in the paint, steps onto his canvas and begins his creation. When he's finished, he steps in a pan of water, washes and dries his feet, puts his painting on the wall and helps someone else paint.

Again, there are prizes for whatever categories you choose: Most Paint, Least Paint, Most Beautiful, Most Colorful, Most Fraught with Meaning, Most Humorous, Etc. Have foot-related prizes: foot powder, foot spray, a ruler, a foot of anything - stickers, ribbon, licorice, etc.

Have everyone sign his creation. Then display them for the rest of the party. Who knows? If you have famous guests, the paintings might be worth something.

People

Any number. This is not a party for your most dignified or dressed up friends. Warn them ahead of time that the event calls for washable clothing.

Environment

Hold this party outdoors, if possible. You'll get fewer grey hairs. If your budget can stand it, visit a paint store and buy paper overalls for everyone. They are only a few dollars and add a great deal of pizzazz to the party. If not overalls, how about berets? You can make them out of whatever fabric you have around. Cut a circle 16" across. Then run a 1/2" hem around it. Run elastic through that hemline and you have a beret of sorts. Certainly enough for people to get the idea. Measure your own head for a gauge for the elastic. Make some larger and some smaller.

Food

To inspire the artists, serve Andy Warhol Soup, Jackson Pollock Pizza, Gauguin Grapes, Foot Long Hot Dogs. If you do serve Foot Long Hot Dogs, fill some of the buns with meatless salad for vegetarians.

Time

Get paint, cookie sheets, butcher paper, paper towels and regular towels; make sure water is available; plan, collect and prepare food; collect prizes.

Special Notes for this Party

Although I only staged this party for adults, it would make a great kid party...*if* you hold it out of doors.

▶ Hootenanny Party

Isn't that a funny word? There's nothing in the world that is more fun than group singing. Although people have been singing forever, it wasn't until the 60s that I heard them called, "Hoots." Whatever you call it, sitting on the floor and singing with your friends is fun.

Event

Group Singing/Hootenannies. A few years ago, nostalgic for a simpler time, I got out my old song books and invited some amateur guitar players and singers like myself for a hootenanny. Some non-guitar players brought percussion instruments while others snapped their fingers or clapped their hands.

If you don't play an instrument, enlist a friend or put a sign up at a nearby college. Offer free food and $25 and you will get a lot of phone calls. Buy or make song books. If you are a bashful singer, invite someone who isn't and ask her to be the leader for the evening.

People

At least two! You can do this with just two people, but everybody likes to sing and since most people have rare opportunities to do it, invite everybody! Find a way to have some version of this party often. When you invite guests, tell them what you have planned and ask if they have any song sheets they want to contribute to the evening. If they're not home when you leave the invite on their answering machine, sing a few bars of "Blowin' in the Wind" as a prelude to the invitation.

Environment

Move all the living room furniture into a circle. Make sure there is plenty of light. Although a campfire sounds great, it's pretty hard to read song books by firelight and it really is more comfortable in the house. Include lots of pillows for floor sitting.

Food

Serve chili, stew, spaghetti or other easy group food. Keep food in some kind of warmer so people can wander in and out for more. Have a big bowl with ice, cans of soda and fruit juices so that guests can help themselves to everything throughout the evening.

Time

Arrange for a guitar player and a song leader, make sure there are song books for everyone, rearrange furniture and get pillows for floor sitting.

Special Notes for this Party

This is a party that the kids like as much as the parents. If the kids are able to read, they will enjoy it, so think of this for a time when you want to entertain family groups.

▶ Tabloid Party

The National Enquirer and The Star magazines are not really publications that I would like to support since I am convinced they make up most of their own material. Here, however, is a what I consider to be the appropriate function of these newspapers: entertainment. It's certainly not credible journalism.

Event

Tabloid Party. A party that goes straight to my heart. Have people come as their favorite real or made-up story from The National Enquirer or The Star, or any of those newspapers that stretch credibility to new limits: "Woman 97 Years Old Gives Birth to Monkey (Father was her pet dog!)" Have prizes for "Most Pathetic Story," "Most Unbelievable," "Most Believable" (that's the booby prize at this party) and so on. Prizes might include copies of (or a subscription to) one of the tabloids or weird toys. Visit magic stores and adult toy stores for ideas. Videotape the stories and show them back to the audience during the food. Polaroids of the participants are great favors to take home.

Guests

At least eight. You want to have enough people to justify everyone else's cleverness. If you want to send invitations rather than just call, visit the newsstand and buy some tabloids. Cut interesting outrageous headlines and arrange them to highlight particulars of the party. If you have pictures of any of your guests, superimpose their faces over those of tabloid subjects. Photocopy and send. Invite guests to bring proof of authenticity: the picture of their monkey offspring, etc. The entertainment at the party will consist of each person telling his story.

Environment

Start collecting copies of these newspapers now for decorations. It will be fun to have all sorts of back issues. Either use the whole newspaper or clip out particularly weird lines and tack them up here and there. Use tabloid headlines on placecards and/or invitations.

Food

Since the aura of such a party is pretty sleazy, serve carny food: popcorn, cotton candy, hot dogs, pizza, etc.

Time

Buy tabloids, make invitations, decorate, buy prizes, plan, gather and prepare food.

Special Notes for this Party

Rent a strobe (to simulate flashbulb effect) from a photography supply store and time it to flash periodically throughout the evening for atmosphere.

Event

Solstice Celebration. June 21, The Longest Day of the Year. Although the Winter and Summer Solstices frequently slip by without any attention paid to them at all, there was a time when these two days were important rituals.

In pagan times, these were the two days of the year on which you took a bath (whether you needed it or not!). Whether or not you will want to feature group bathing to commemorate that event is your business, but if you do, June 21 is the day on which to celebrate the longest day of the year.

Invite guests to wear "long" johns, "long" pants, or "long" skirts. Really enthusiastic folk will want to wear all three.

Tell guests there will be prizes for jokes, stories, and/or tall tales. Give prizes for Longest Funny Jokes, Longest Stupid Jokes, Most Stupid Long Joke, Longest Joke, Shortest Long Joke, Biggest Stretch. The possibilities are endless. If you clue guests in to categories for awards, this will stimulate their imaginations when sifting their brains for story possibilities.

For prizes give long pencils, long skinny tablets, long-burning candles, visit a second-hand bookstore for The Loneliness of the Long Distance Runner and other titles featuring the word "long."

Who Am I is a fun choice. The game goes like this: When the guest arrives, the host pins a sign with a famous person's name on it to each guest's back. The other guests, of course, can read the sign. In order to find out who you are, you ask questions that can be answered "yes" or "no" like "Am I living?" or "Am I a writer?" and so on. You can only ask two questions of the same person and then must move on and ask someone else.

This is an effective way to get people talking to one another. Adapt the game to this party by featuring tall people or those who have the word "Long" in their names: "Long"fellow, Wilt Chamberlain, "Long" John Silver, Icabod Crane, Olive Oyl, Kareem Abdul-Jabbar, etc.

The highlight of the evening is when the sun finally goes down. Give everyone sparklers to light to mark the darkness. It's all uphill after this day. The days will only get shorter.

Play **Long Charades.** Use all kinds of long titles and titles with the word "long" in them. Songs: "It's a Long, Long Trail A Winding," "The Long and Winding Road," "Long Ago and Far Away," etc. Movies: "The Long Long Long Long Trailer," "The Long Goodbye," "The Longest Day," etc.

At the end of the evening, when you give awards for jokes, stories, whatever, be sure the ribbons are very *long!*

Guests

Any number. This is a party best held outside for the full celebration of daylight. Make sure you leave a "long" message when you leave the invitation on the answering machine. Keep calling back the machine and leaving more details.

Environment

Decorate with "long" calendars made by taping all the pages of calendars end to end so that the entire year is viewed at once. Use a *long* roll of toilet paper as a garland. Make sure not to break it and display it going from room to room and through doorways. Feature music with the word "long" in the title: "Long Ago and Far Away," "It's a Long Long Trail A Winding," music from the show, <u>Take Me Along</u>. Also display books with "long" in the title.

Food

For dinner, serve extra-"long" spaghetti, "long"-grained rice, "long" sandwiches, etc. Dessert suggestions include "long" strands of licorice, "long" cakes made by splitting rectangular cakes and joining them end to end before frosting.

Time

Make signs for *Who Am I?* game, prepare material for Charades, get prizes.

Special Notes for this Party

Make a point of having a "long" party by turning this into a sleepover or if the calendar cooperates, a weekend party.

► Circus Party

One of the best parties I ever went to was a *Circus Party*. Everyone was invited to come as a circus act. There were all the standard things: Bareback Riders, Lion Tamers, etc. Some couples came as Siamese Twins.

Event

The Greatest Show in Walnut Grove (or wherever you live). The party was in the summer and took place in the backyard. Trapezes were hung from the trees as well as one of those long ropes that women cling to high above the crowd at the circus. I don't think anyone will be tempted to use these props, but to ward off insurance problems, remind people they can't use them without an "Acrobat's License."

The hosts had rented a life-size paper-mache elephant. Guests climbed the ladder and had their picture taken on the elephant alone or with others. If you can't come up with an elephant, maybe you'll come up with a pony. Be sure to decorate his saddle and bridle.

There were carny-type games to play: ring toss, dropping clothes pins in milk bottles, etc., and, of course, prizes for those games as well as prizes for costumes. For your party, visit second-hand stores for old circus posters to add to the atmosphere.

People

At least eight. Ask each guest to prepare a contribution to "The Main Event" by being a sword swallower, fire-eater, magician, etc. Have ideas to suggest when you issue the invitation. Keep track so you won't end up with five jugglers. At the party I attended, all the tricks were wonderfully phony and stupid, but treated with great respect. The party was only twelve guests large but we all had a colossal time. Each guest got a helium-filled balloon as a favor. There were prizes for Best Act, Shortest, Funniest, Most Daring, etc.

Environment

Hang trapezes from the trees (too high for temptation), climbing ropes, helium-filled balloons, crepe paper, big posters, circus posters. Get carousel music as well as the music from <u>Carnival</u> for background.

Food

Circus food: pizza, hot dogs, peanuts, popcorn; for the vegetarians serve shish kebabs of grilled vegetables. Have ice cream cones and cotton candy for dessert.

Time

Plan and procure game materials; plan, collect and prepare food; get helium-filled balloons; plan show and assign parts.

Special Notes for this Party

The first thought is to make this elaborate and luxurious (***The Greatest Show in Walnut Grove***), but, maybe the most fun is to be as seedy and tacky as you can think of. Call it ***Smith's Last Chance Circus.***

► Happy Birthday Fido/Fluffy Party

My agent, Rick Axe, gave a fabulous birthday when his dog, Gummy Bear, was one year old. Ric invited 16 of his best "dog" friends (16 friends of Rick's who had dogs). The party was held in the park and everyone thought it was hilarious.

Event

Happy Birthday Fido/Fluffy. Held on your pet's birthday. You may want to fudge a little on the date if it falls in the dead of winter. Rick's party was adorable. There were party hats for all the dogs (Gummy Bear wore a fireman's hat). Rick bought a dog-shaped piñata and filled it with dog treats, dog chewies and other toys. He hired a clown who made balloon animals and balloon doggie hats for all the guests, four-legged and otherwise.

The "party dogs" got a little nervous as the piñata was being broken, but when the "goods were spilled in the grass," dogs came from all over the park! This year, as favors he is featuring bandannas printed with Gummy Bear's name, birth date, and party date.

Guests

Only invite your friends with dogs. At least five.

Environment

Drape crepe paper from trees and hang big pictures of Lassie and/or the guest of honor.

Food

Gourmet dog food for the canine guests, pizza for the humans. Have a cake in the shape of a bone and have a tray brimming over with doggie chews in the shape of doggie tacos, cannolis, etc.

Time

Buy and stuff piñata, hire clown, get balloons, buy doggie party hats, get doggie chews in food shapes, order pizza, arrange for gourmet dog food, order or bake cake.

Special Notes for this Party

Have a weather back-up day. Allow time at the beginning of the party for the dogs to get used to each other and calm down. Many of them may not be that used to seeing other dogs. Check with owners to make sure their dogs are friendly and non-combative.

▶ Slumber Parties

For a long time I've had this fantasy that I wanted all my women friends to come and spend the weekend. Finally, this year, as a late birthday present to myself and one of my best friends, I invited eight friends for a party.

Event

Ladies Weekend. I started this party in stages because it's hard to find people who can commit enough time to a whole weekend. Friday night, my friend, Donna, came in from San Francisco. She's a great party organizer, too, so we had a good time putting the finishing touches together. We were looking for something interesting to do with the *"Who Am I?"* game to tailor it to this party, when we realized that the next day was Ground Hog's Day. We giggled and giggled as we decided that all the "Who Am I?" signs would feature elusive people. We used Greta Garbo, Lamont Cranston (The Shadow), Howard Hughes, the Unknown Soldier, etc.

Saturday morning, we had a cast of six for brunch. I had gone to the crafts store the day before to buy supplies for *Colors*, a game that turned out to be the highlight of the weekend.

I bought lots of tissue paper in terrific colors. As each guest arrived, I asked her to choose two pieces of paper: one which symbolized how she feels most of the time, and the second for how she thinks others perceive her. Then everyone tore a hole in the center of the paper making a kind of sandwich-board effect and put the "true" color tissue on first and the "cover" color on second.

As people got drinks and mingled, we all talked about why we chose the colors and what that meant to us. It was interesting on many levels. I had chosen yellow as my "cover" color because I think that is how people perceive me: "cheerful, sunny." My friend, Georgann had chosen the same "cover" color for herself for entirely different reasons. She said she found yellow "jarring" and felt that is how people perceive her.

These conversations carried us through brunch and into many other different areas. After we all did the dishes, we gathered in the living room for the second part of the game. Now it was time for each guest to find out how, in fact, others really did perceive her. The perceiv*ers* said things like, "Well, you may think people see you as "purple", but I see "red" because you have so much fire and energy..." To demonstrate they tore or cut tissue paper in other colors and taped them to the "cover" color.

After *Colors* was finished, we took a long walk together. When we returned home, everyone worked together to prepare supper. As the two remaining guests arrived, Donna and I pinned the "Who Am I?" papers to everyone's back and we played as we prepared supper. Georgann had asked if she could bring the favors for the party. They were wrapped in fabulous colors of tissue and tied with paper ribbon. As we gathered at the table, finding our presents started us on another round of excitement that carried over into the meal. After the dishes were done we played ***Rummy Royal.*** The next morning after a walk and Brunch, my friends all left. We had such a good time, it's going to be a bi-annual event.

Rummy Royal

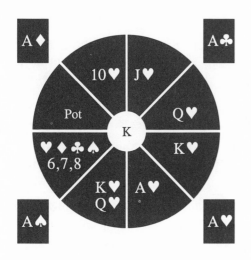

Rummy Royal is a terrific game. The only thing you have to remember about this game is to be alert. If you don't pay attention, you won't get to collect your money! No second chances. I love this game. It is a combination of many games and requires a game board that I always make myself. It's sometimes called Michigan Rummy or Tripoli and as such is available in toy stores with their set of rules and a game board. I learned the game 30 years ago in Texas with a made-up game board and have been playing it that way ever since. The optimal number of players is eight. You can play with poker chips, pennies, nickels, or dimes. I'm too nervous to play for more than pennies. Ask each guest to bring 300 pennies to the game. The game board is a circle that is divided into 13 spaces (as per illustration). Use a rectangular piece of poster board about 36" x 24". You can either draw cards on it or do as I do and cannibalize an old deck of cards. As you can see, there are 13 areas that include: 10,J,Q,K,A ♥; another A ♥; and another KQ ♥; one each of the other Aces: ♦,♣,♠; a picture of a "kitty"; another of "the pot." The last space is taken by the "money space" that doesn't come up too often: 6-7-8 ♥, 6-7-8 ♦, 6-7-8♣, and 6-7-8-♠. That money is paid when you have (and get to play) the 6-7-8 of the same suit. More about that later. Each player will begin each game by putting a penny (or a poker chip) on each space, so it costs each player 13 pennies to play each game.

Although the game seems complicated when you are learning it, I promise that after a few hands, everything I am about to tell you will become automatic. Just begin following the directions. Don't read all the directions first. Just start going through the motions as you read them. Everyone ante up. Each player must put one penny on each "money space." Make sure each player puts in her pennies. The dealer will now deal 8 hands with an extra one for herself. This is one more hand than there are players. The hands will not all have the same number of cards. Don't worry. These things work out.

It all starts with "The Auction." The dealer takes the last hand dealt herself and does *not* look at the other hand. All the other players look at their hands and each decides if they like the hand they were dealt or would like to bid on the "extra" hand. The decision is made based on whether or not the hands contain any "money" cards (high ♥ or Aces) or if the best 5 cards (some will have more cards) might comprise a winning poker hand. The dealer is now in control. She can either keep the unseen extra hand herself (if she doesn't like her hand) or she can auction *that hand* sight unseen. If she does keep it, she burns the old hand by putting it face down on "the kitty" in the center of the board. If the new hand is worse than her first hand, too bad, she's stuck. If she does sell the hand, she starts with the person to her left and says, "Would you like to buy this hand?" The bidding starts there and goes around the table with people dropping out and the highest bidder taking the hand. Sometimes the hand goes for one penny and sometimes it goes for 75 cents or more. That money goes to the dealer. Once the hand has been auctioned, it's time for phase two.

The next part of the game is Poker. Now the person to the left of the dealer opens for Poker. You don't have to be a Poker player for this part of the game. I type up four lists of the winning hands and have them strategically placed around the table for inexperienced Poker players. If you don't know Poker, you will catch on pretty quickly. In this particular Poker game, you do not show your cards when you win because, not only do you not want people to know what you have for the other parts of the game, but, people will see what you have as you play those cards down on the table later. You can bluff, but you cannot lie. High pairs frequently win in a game of 8 players because you do not get to draw for extra cards. Poker antes go into the "kitty" so the winner gets not only the proceeds of the Poker but all the pennies already in the kitty from the ante.

The third part of the game is "Collecting Your Aces." Once Poker has been won (and only now) anyone who has an Ace may collect the money on the corresponding Ace in the *corners*. If you have the Ace of ♣, you get that money. Part of the fun is when someone forgets to collect her ace, so don't tell. Just take your money quietly if you have an Ace and hope you get the uncollected Ace next time when there will be twice as much money on it. The "Aces" phase of the game goes very quickly as the person who won at Poker (who collects her Ace and/or gives a brief moment for everyone else to collect) now starts the play of the game. By taking her lowest black card (Aces are high), she places it in front of her and calls out: "Two of ♣" or "7 of ♠" or whatever. There is no choice, you must play your lowest black card. Whoever has the next card in sequence takes it from her hand, calls out "three of ♣" and plays it faceup in front of herself for all to see. This continues until no one has the next card. This happens a lot because one hand has been burned. If you play the "5♠" and no one has the 6♠, you then switch to your lowest *red* card and call it out. When the 10♥ is played, that player takes the money that is on that card, and so on. If you have the Q♥ and K♥, you collect on Q♥, K♥ and on the Q/K♥ space.

At some point, whether the "money cards" come up or not, someone will run out of cards and "go out." At that point, she quickly hollers, "I'm out" before anyone collects any other money cards and puts her hand out to collect one penny from each player for every card they have left in their hand. She also gets the money in the pot. If she forgets "the pot" then the next person who goes out gets double money. Once the hand is over, everybody antes up and the game starts once again. Since the Q/K♥ and the 6-7-8 (of the same suit) don't come up very often, the money collects on those spaces and becomes quite sizable by the end of the evening. At the end of the evening, all money left on the board is grouped together and you play 5 cards dealt face up in front of each player one at a time. The highest hand wins.

A general word: at all phases of the game, if someone forgets to pick up money at the appropriate time, they cannot collect it late. If their hand is in the act of reaching, that's okay, for we know they did not forget. This includes the "pot" that you collect at the end of a round or the Poker winnings (the Pot) or the corner Aces and/or the ♥ money cards. Remember, the A♥ in the center is collected only when that A is played during the play of the game. All money not collected per each hand just builds and the next person gets double or triple, depending on how long it has been since someone won that space.

People

Eight is the best number, but adjust it to your friends and how much space you have to bed people down.

Environment

Since this is a whole weekend and there is so much to be done, I wouldn't bother with any kinds of decorations. Just putting fresh flowers in every room is enough. If you don't have lots of beds, have people bring bed rolls. Once when I went to a party like this at someone's beach house with many more people than rooms, there were bed rolls everywhere: on the patio, on the sand, in the living room, wherever. If you need your privacy, just choose an empty corner out of the traffic pattern.

Food

My fantasy had us sharing in the food preparation equally, but, I was very content to have everyone pitch in as though they lived there so that I wasn't really on duty. One of the guests suggested that the next time we should rent a cabin someplace, share the cost and each can be responsible for a different meal. In that case, choose food that's not too complicated as everyone will be bringing ingredients. Under those conditions, Saturday night's meal, at a restaurant, will give everyone a change of venue.

Time

Buy tissue paper. Get *Who Am I?* game together. Make signs. Be sure you have straight pins. Make sure guests like to play cards and are prepared to bring (and possibly *lose*) 300 pennies. Have bowls or jars ready for people to put their pennies in. Make or buy the game board. When people ask what they can bring, say, "Nothing. Just help me when you're here so I can be a guest, too."

Special Notes for this Party

Be sure to have a terrific favor for the guests to take home. If you have the money to do it, have T-shirts printed that say something like, "Mary's Weekend" with the date. Be sure to take pictures. You can hand them out at the next party!

Event

This weekend is every bit as good an idea for men as it is for women, although probably not as necessary since guys seem to find time to play together all the time anyway. They don't usually spend weekends together, though, so what the heck. Gather everyone on Friday night for Poker. Guys bond differently than women, so just plunge in with the game. Have dinner first or have a deli spread, veggies, dips, hot dogs, hamburgers, or whatever other finger foods, plus beer, sodas and juices available throughout the game. Losers are responsible for breakfast. After breakfast, take a walk to buy supplies for dinner and come back and make lunch.

In the afternoon head for the basketball hoop and shoot a little "One-on-One" or "Horse." Whatever you play, have prizes. They can either be gag prizes or something nice like Robert Bly's book, <u>A Gathering of Men</u>.

Have everyone cook dinner together. Afterwards, play the game I just described for the Women's Slumber Party, Rummy Royal.

People

Eight is best, but accommodate your list of friends.

Environment

Bed rolls if needed. If you live in an area where the surroundings and weather permit, you might all want to sleep in the backyard. In any event, have food and drinks available around the clock. It doesn't all have to be chips and beer, even if it is for guys.

Food

Have "finger-food" on Friday night: deli-spread, veggies, dip, nachos, pizza, hot dogs, burgers, etc. Set out cereals, toppings, milk, coffee, etc. for breakfast. Poker's losers are fixing. Saturday night eat out. Sunday morning fix pancakes with lots of toppings.

Time

Make Rummy Royal board. Make sure everyone brings pennies. Have containers for people to put them in. Get the food for Friday night. Lay in extra toothbrushes in case anyone forgets. Get food supplies. Decide on a restaurant (or have choices available) for Saturday night. Find a place to shoot baskets and make sure you have a basketball.

Special Notes for this Party

Give everyone a t-shirt printed "International Games" (or whatever) for everyone. Get half one color and half another for the team games.

► Winter Solstice Party

I've always known about Winter Solstice, but it never occurred to me to celebrate it until I found myself performing in a play in Alaska. If you don't celebrate the solstice in Alaska, you never will.

Event

Winter Solstice Party. December 21, The Shortest Day of the Year. When Alaskans talk about the shortest day of the year, they're not kidding around. In Anchorage we had six hours of daylight that day.

To celebrate the shortest day I ever saw, I gave a "short" party "shortly" before the play to which everyone was invited to wear "short" skirts or "shorts." Guests were invited to prepare a "short joke, skit, poem, speech," etc.

If you tell people ahead of time what the prizes will be given for (Wittiest, Shortest, Most Obscure, Most Emotional, etc.) this information will inspire their choices. Give tiny books, toys, decks of cards, etc.

We also played *Short Who Am I?* (the game that adapts to any party.) The game goes like this. When the guest arrives, the host pins a sign with a famous person's name on it to the guest's back. The other guests, of course, can read the sign. In order to find out who you are, you ask questions that can be answered "yes" or "no": "Am I living?" or "Am I a writer?" or "Am I female?" and so on. You can only ask two questions of the same person and then must move on and ask someone else. It's a fun way to get people talking to one another. At this party, all the names belonged to short people. We had Dustin Hoffman, Toulouse Lautrec, Dudley Moore, Linda Hunt, Napoleon, etc.

Guests

Any number. Best is eight to ten. Send "short" notes for invitations if you use hard copy, leave "short" messages on answering machines. For best effect, have the party at sundown (that could be early).

Environment

Feature clocks, calendars, sundials, timers and anything else you can think of that has to do with time.

Food

We served "short" ribs, shrimp, new potatoes, baby vegetables, "shortbread" cookies and strawberry "shortcake."

Time

Prepare signs for *Who Am I.* Get miniature prizes; plan, collect and prepare food; decorate.

Special Notes for this Party

Measure all guests at the end of the party and give a prize to the shortest one. Give a framed picture of Mickey Rooney with a forged personalized message: *"To Mary: from one terrific short person to another. You were swell. Mickey."*

Some people are intimidated by Trivial Pursuit thinking they don't know enough to play well. Solve the problem by playing in teams.

Event

Trivial Pursuit and Variations. One needs to have a similar-thinking group for Trivial Pursuit. My son Jamie's attitude toward the game is very serious. He doesn't like to play with people who bend the rules. I, on the other hand, want to make sure the game does not go on forever. I vary the rules by allowing a player who has already collected a blue piece of pie (or red, yellow, etc.) to collect a different colored piece next time he answers a questions correctly. This way, players can fill in the 6 colored pieces of pie much sooner. If you've got lots of really smart trivia folks, they will want to play it by the book. Play the game any way you prefer, it's always fun. It's also informative.

Just as in Pictionary, I prefer to have two teams of many players. This way you don't wait so long between turns.

If you want to do more than just invite people to dinner and break out the Trivial Pursuit game afterwards, spot trivia questions all over the house, add some to the placecards at the table. Tape old TV themes (there's a collection called Tee Vee Toons you can get at any record store that's perfect for this) for use as background music. Later, ask questions about the music people have been listening to all night.

Make up trivia questions about guests. Ask questions based on current events: sports, financial, political, etc.

Use the same ideas to create your own *Trivial Charades*.

Guests

At least four. Include a made-up trivia question with your invitation whether you send it via the mail or an answering machine. If they answer the phone, tell them you're conducting a quiz and if they can answer the trivia question, they get a prize. Then ask a question you know the guest can answer (be sure to have it prepared ahead of time).

141

When they answer correctly, tell them they have won a free dinner and an evening to pit their skills against some of the sharpest minds in the city. When everyone arrives, give each an index card on which are written several trivia questions which they must ask other guests to answer, i.e.: *"How many people at this party were born in December?"* *"How many people at this party drive an American car?"* and so on. Make sure you have five different questions for each guest.

Environment

Spot trivia questions (from the game, and personal ones pertinent to the guests) through out the house. Be sure to have several cards on the wall in the bathroom. Things like: *"How much toilet paper does an average guest use?"* etc. On placecards have a trivia question about food. Old TV themes for music. See above.

Food

Whatever you choose to serve, find trivia questions to ask about different items and put a folded card under each plate with a different question i.e., *"Is a tomato a fruit, or a vegetable?"* (Answer: fruit); *"In it's natural state, does chocolate taste a) salty b) sweet c) bitter or d) sour?"* (Answer: Chocolate is extremely bitter until sugar is added); "If you accidentally oversalt a dish, what can you add to correct your mistake?" (Answer: Potatoes. They absorb the salt). Other questions: *"What was Julia Child's first cookbook?"* (Answer: Mastering the Art of French Cooking); *"Which contains more calories, an average size apple or banana?"* (Answer: banana). For other interesting trivia on all subjects, check In Search of Trivia by Jeff Rovin (Signet Books). This is an invaluable sourcebook for information to put in various games.

Time

Get Trivial Pursuit, make up *Trivial Pursuit Charades* and food trivia for placecards. Plan, gather and prepare food. Tape old TV themes.

Special Notes for this Party

This is a party that lends itself to weekly or monthly gatherings that float from house to house. The host can prepare food or each guest can bring a dish. That way it's not too much trouble for anyone.

> ▶ **National Hippie Day**
> **Woodstock Weekend**

August 17-19, 1969 marks the date of the most historic love-in of all time: The Infamous Woodstock Weekend. This is the perfect time to remember the hope and idealism of an earlier era. Also a great time to dust off those old bell-bottom pants you've been saving just in case they come "in" again.

Event

National Hippie Day. Celebrate on the Saturday closest to August 17th or go for it and stage your own weekend love-in. Whether you opt for one night or more, have a '60s Hootenanny, play '60s Charades, and participate in '60s Arts and Crafts.

For prizes, give flowers, make head bands, and tie-dye old t-shirts. Give prizes for Most Idealistic Guest, Most Laid Back, Best Protest Poster, Best "Love-child", etc. Encourage guests to dress '60s.

My favorite part of this party is the group singing featuring songs like: "This Land Is Your Land," "If I Had A Hammer," "We Shall Overcome," "Blowin' In the Wind," etc.

You'll need at least one guitar player (the more the better) and a confident leader/singer. If you or a friend don't play guitar, a note on a nearby college or high school bulletin board should yield at least one guitar player who will be happy to make $25 to play and sing and eat with you and your friends.

Singalongs are only successful when all the singers know the words to all the songs. Visit a music store, buy a collection of '60s songs and hand them out when the singing starts. Alphabetize and number the songs so that when someone spots an old favorite and wants the crowd to sing it, all they have to do is shout out the number and everyone can find it easily.

'60s Charades features timely quotes, slogans, and events for material: "Hair," "I Have a Dream," "Give Peace A Chance," "Don't Trust Anyone Over 30," etc.

People

Any number. No conservatives. When guests arrive, put a string of love beads around their neck and give them a kiss or if each guest is to make her own necklace, give her a kiss and point her towards the beads as soon as she walks in the door.

Environment

Have a table with beads, colored string and colored markers and paper for drawing peace signs, flowers, protest slogans, etc. A neighborhood arts and crafts store can supply everything you'll need.

Go to the library and photocopy newspaper articles about the Civil Rights Marches, Anti-Vietnam Marches, and, of course, Woodstock. Put them on the wall along side your own family pictures of that era.

Food

Vegetarianism was an important factor during the '60s so a vegetarian menu will contribute to the ambience. Let people assemble their own pita sandwiches from sprouts, guacamole, egg salad, pasta salad, tomatoes, onions and dressings. Don't forget brown rice. Have brownies for dessert!

Time

Set up work table; gather beads, string, markers, flowers, paper, cardboard and other craft supplies; assemble '60s song sheets; prepare *'60s Charades*, get guitar player; go to library to research and photocopy articles; gather, prepare and assemble food.

Special Notes for this Party

To set the mood further, go to your local used book or thrift stores and, for practically nothing, you can get magazines from the '60s. For a special treat, get magazines like <u>Look</u>, that are now extinct. Period music, newspapers, peace signs, poster size personal photos. Love beads for favors.

Life's Other Events
Birthdays/Anniversaries

4   Life's Other Events
Birthdays/Anniversaries

Since Birthdays and Anniversaries are specifically about celebrating *numbers*, it's fun to plan parties and presents around them. Certain birthdays are special and it's fun to mark them with "16," "21," "30" or "50" of something: dollars, balloons, lottery tickets, etc. The following ideas can be adapted to birthdays or anniversaries. There are elements in each that might appeal to you, so read all of them and use those most appropriate for your occasion.

Event

"For Landmark Birthdays up to Age 40." Celebrate the passage of "youth" by presenting black armbands to all the guests and spraying their hair with (washable) grey haircolor. This year my daughter turned 30 and, even though there were only four of us at the party, spraying our hair made for a hilarious evening. We decorated with black balloons and ribbons.

I found some great kites which I used for decoration and gave as favors. In memory of "younger times," we jumped rope and played jacks.

People

Any number. I wouldn't want to give away my fun idea beforehand, but make sure your guests will be good sports and are not folk who spend $50 to get their hair done just before a party. If you want to send hard copy invitations, you might send something somber either edged in black, with a black ribbon as trim, or the black armbands you want them to wear. Say something like:

"In memory of the passage of Mary's youth (she's turning 30, after all), we are gathering to remember the past and ponder the future. Friday, March 30 at 7:30 p.m. exactly. Dress for childish activities. Please wear a black armband. RSVP by March 25 to 213-555-5555."

Environment

Resurrect the appropriate childhood days by recreating some of the things that were happening at that time. Invite guests to come in period clothing.

Food

Serve the birthday person's favorite food or peanut butter and jelly sandwiches, Ritz or Honey Gram crackers and chocolate milk "in memory" of youthful times.

Special Notes for this Party

This is one of those occasions when a camcorder is a must. If you don't own one, borrow one. Historic birthdays should be preserved.

Event

"Landmark Birthdays Older than 40"/Second Childhood. We all have an age threshold that suddenly means "old" to us. Make sure you know what that is for the guest of honor and be sensitive to it. Birthday cards featuring wrinkles, sags and bags are fun to some but pretty depressing to others. My father is 86, and I don't think he's one bit happy about not being 30 any more than I am. Once past 40, celebrate how young the person still is. Feature the past in the most optimistic way (recall accomplishments) and the future (future plans or predictions). Choose a childhood villain (political, cartoon, school principal, etc.), enlarge a photo and throw darts.

Another idea is to choose a fad from the time (Hula-Hoop, Charleston, whatever) for featured entertainment.

Guests

Any number. Miss Manners says that even if you *don't* want people to bring presents it is inappropriate to even mention gifts. That being the situation, it's not necessary to announce that the occasion is a birthday unless this is a family gathering, in which case, people will be bringing presents anyway. If you were planning any kind of activity where a particular kind of dress is required, specify that. Otherwise, just invite guests to the party and let them discover when they get there that it is a significant birthday.

For an unusual memento for the guest of honor, put a basket by the front door filled with lovely smooth stones and colored markers. Select the number of stones to correspond with the event. Invite guests to write good wishes (*"Health," "Happiness," "50 more wonderful years,"* etc.) on the stones. Then spray them with spray net or polyurethane so the thoughts are preserved and present them to the guest of honor in the basket.

Check the yellow pages under "rocks" for a source.

Environment

Feature pictures of the guest of honor at various ages. Report cards and other mementos from the past are fun decorations. I've had pictures from my childhood Brownie camera enlarged to poster size. They turned out great! Feature musical milestones from the guest's past. "The Wedding March," "Pomp and Circumstance," etc. If it's an anniversary, be sure to feature "their" song as well as "The Anniversary Waltz."

Food

Even if you don't serve champagne throughout the evening, at least have it, or sparkling cider, for the toast. Since turkey is mainly served only at Thanksgiving or Christmas, it's thought of as a sort of "occasion" dish. Pair it with wild rice and it's a whole different experience. Serve your favorite green salad, vegetable and cranberry sauce. Alternatives to traditional birthday cake are cookies, ice cream or yogurt parfaits with candles stuck in them.

Special Notes for this Party

Since the *Crayola Day party* is also childhood-themed, it could be adapted for this occasion.

Anniversaries are sentimental occasions whether it is your parent's 50th or your 5th.

Event

Your Anniversary. Anniversaries are so personal that I'm just going to list some ideas. If you have the money, rent a limousine or a luxury car for the day. In Los Angeles, you can even rent a tank! Picnic in the afternoon and go to "your" restaurant at night.

On their anniversary, a friend of mine told her husband to prepare for surprises all day long. They had brunch at a swank hotel and then went off to a romantic movie and dinner.

Another friend (a wonderfully outrageous one) surprised her husband by renting a room for the night at a lovely hotel. She visited early in the day and placed their overnight belongings and other personal objects as though they lived there. She took her husband to the hotel for dinner and afterwards, cajoled him into a walk through the grounds. She had left the door ajar to their bungalow and as they passed it, she said, *"Oh, let's go in!"* Her husband was having a conniption as she unbuttoned her blouse and pulled him inside. It took him a moment to realize their things were in the room and it was perfectly all right. It was so "wicked" and one of their best anniversaries. They both told me.

Event

Your Parent's Anniversary. Adult children frequently honor their parents on significant anniversaries: 25, 50, 75, or anywhere in between. Whether these parties are held at home or at a restaurant, decorate with pictures from the wedding, if possible. Have the bridal picture copied into a wall size poster. As guests arrive, give them a pencil and an index card and ask them each to write something they remember about the couple. Later, quiet the group and have each person read his card.

Have a scrap book with plastic sleeves to collect the cards as a memento. If you have a camcorder, now's the time. Tape all the guests and their tributes.

► Showers

Baby Showers, Wedding Showers, Etc. There are all sorts of clever things to do at showers. Although opening of presents is a focal point, it adds to the party to play a game or two and if you can afford it, hire a psychic. It's lots of fun and contributes to the sense of silliness. Whether you're celebrating a wedding, a divorce or a baby, everyone gets a kick out of "inside information."

Event

The Wedding Shower. Increasingly this shower is for both the bride and groom. Whether it is coed or not, plan some fun games so the party is not just about opening presents. An informative and fun wedding shower game to play is *Wedding Information.* Give each guest a paper and pencil to write down *"Ten Things Married People Fight About."* After the food is served, have each guest read her list. Give a prize for the Funniest, Weirdest, and Most Informative Lists.

Another interesting thing to do is to stage your own version of television's *"Newlyweds"* game. Feature only the engaged couple or choose two or three couples to compete with them. Ask questions like they do on the show: *"What is your mate's favorite color?" "What is your mate's favorite food?" "If your mate were stranded on a desert island, what book would he/she take with him?" "What food?"* Remember, these people are getting married soon and they're under stress, so don't give them an excuse to fight by getting too intimate.

Adapt any of the games we have spoken about in other parties to the shower occasion. *Who Am I?* for a wedding shower features famous wives (Raiza Gorbachev, Nancy Reagan, Zsazsa Gabor, Ivana Trump, etc.) If it's a kitchen shower, feature famous chefs (Julia Child, Paul Prudhomme, Wolfgang Puck, Chef Boyardee, etc.)

Another bridal shower game is *Wisdom*. Tell everyone at the beginning of the party that they'll be asked to make a list of five wise sayings for the bride and groom after dinner. After dessert, when the lists are made and gathered, have the bride and groom alternate reading the advice.

Guests give stupid advice and funny advice and maybe even wise advice. Have them sign their offerings. Give prizes for "Most Helpful," "Wisest," "Funniest," etc. If you announce categories ahead of time, it will give guests inspiration for their lists.

Buy a photograph album with clear sleeves and put all the advice in the album (provide colored cards for guests to write on that are the appropriate size). The album will make a nice present for the bride and groom.

Guests

At least five close friends of the couple. Hard copy invitations can include tiny umbrellas or plastic rain bonnets.

Environment

Make banners with Real or Phony Folk Advice to the bride or groom: *"Remember that a little black shoe polish rubbed between his toes insures fidelity," "Salt sprinkled in the right shoe on the wedding day insures a long and happy marriage."*

Food

Have pasta with sun dried tomatoes and basil, serve a great Caesar salad, garlic bread and traditional "Shower Tea Cakes" from a bakery for dessert.

Special Notes for this Party

Help the guest(s) of honor by keeping track of the presents and who they are from.

Event

Baby Shower. Baby showers are traditionally held just prior to the baby's arrival. Be sure to find out from "mommy" what she needs as many people will ask you when you issue the invitation. Game possibilities include: ***Baby Trivial Pursuit*** or ***Baby Charades***. These games can be informative and/or silly, depending on what facts you choose to feature. Look up statistics about babies, for example, *"43% of all the babies born last year were boys."* Feature made-up things babies might say: *"Heh, heh, heh, they think I'm asleep," "She thinks I'm going to eat **this**?,"* etc.

Play ***Baby Wisdom.*** Give card and pencil to each guest. Ask them to make up five serious or funny pieces of advice for "Mom and Dad": *"Be good to this child, she will be supporting you in your old age!" "If a child does not eat sugar until her 16th birthday - she may be healthy but she will also be very very cranky!"* etc. Give prizes for Funniest, Best, Shortest, Longest, etc.

Make baby bonnets for all the guests to wear. Use cardboard and glue cotton flannel to the finished product. A shamrock is really the same shape as a baby's bonnet, if you think about it. Just put your head where the stem goes, so use that shape as your guide. Staple or glue ribbon to hold it on. Everyone will look adorable. Paint rattles with each guests' name and use for placecards.

Guests

Any number. Get a list of "mom's" best friends.

Environment

Get a dozen baby bottles (give them to "mom" afterwards) and fill with M&M's, red hots, tootsie rolls, jelly beans, flowers, etc. Put them on tables and/or use them as a centerpiece. For music play "What's the Matter With Kids Today?" "Go to Sleepy, Little Baby," "Rock-a-by My Baby," "Baby, It's Cold Outside," etc.

Food

Serve cheese souffle, salad, croissants, baby carrots, and have fresh fruit on puff pastry for dessert.

Special Notes for this Party

Be sure to list all the presents and their source for the busy "mommy."

► Divorce/Leaving Home Showers

Event

The Divorce Shower/Leaving Home Party. Sad but true, people do split up sometimes and often one half of the couple is left high and dry without any supplies. And sometimes, when friends finally "leave home," they find themselves having to set up a whole house without Mom and Dad's vacuum cleaner, pie pan, coffee pot, etc. so it's fun and thoughtful to throw a party for those folk and "shower" them with a few necessities.

Guests

Any number. Eight is best.

Environment

If you can get your hands on a picture of the bride and groom, tear the pictures in half. Pair your friend with a great catch and pair the "other" half with someone less than desirable. Play "broken heart," "he/she did me dirty" music: "Your Cheating Heart," "For the Good Times," "You Don't Bring Me Flowers," "It's My Party and I'll Cry If I Want To," etc. Play *Divorce Charades* using titles like: "What Did I Have That I Don't Have," "How Could I Believe You When You Said You Loved Me When I Know You've Been a Liar All My Life,""I Must Have Been Out of my Mind," "Sadder But Wiser," etc.

Food

Have a Saturday morning Brunch. Serve Chile Rellenos. It's easy and delicious. Have a green salad, soft warm flour tortillas, and guacamole. For dessert have crisp flour tortillas covered with sour cream and sprinkled with assorted sliced fresh fruit (strawberries, blueberries, peach, kiwi).

158

Special Notes for this Party

It's difficult and sad to be starting all over, and scary for newly divorced, so make the party as light and silly as possible. At the end of the party, all join hands and pledge support for each other. Have each guest write her phone number on an address label (the kind that are pressure sensitive) and stick it on the guest of honor as she leaves saying, *"Hey, call me if you need anything!"*

▶ Distant Family Parties

Today so many of us live long distances (either geographically *or* emotionally) from our families that when we get together on State Occasions, it's frequently awkward. Everyone leads such divergent lives that once all non-present members of the family have been discussed, there's not a lot to do. Even if you have come together for a birthday or Christmas, the atmosphere can be a little strained until present opening time. These are just the occasions that call for imagination and good humor.

Event

Distant Family Parties. First of all, if you don't have one, go out and buy a terrific brightly colored jigsaw puzzle and have it out, with the border already worked, and ready for people to work on. Don't get one that is too easy or it will be used up too quickly, and don't get one that is too hard and doesn't even inspire you to try. If you don't have a spare table, get a piece of plywood that's big enough to accommodate the puzzle, it's box and lots of elbows. Lay it out on top of another table in the living room where there is good light and lots of chairs.

To get people started on the puzzle, have one particular space you are trying to fill in and ask for help there. It takes a few minutes to get people interested, and it's only a device to free people from "having" to find something to talk about right away. Once everyone has gathered and is working at the puzzle, you'll find that tensions will ease.

During the meal, you can sneak in a little game of *Family History Trivia* by using placecards with a "Family Trivia" question at each place. Ask things that bring up happy family history. *"What was your first grade teacher's name?" "What is the first thing you can remember eating that you loved?" "What is the best thing you can remember about when you were little?" "If you could change one thing about your childhood, what would it be?"* and so on.

At dessert time, have everyone turn her placecard over (use an inverted "V" so you can write inside it and no one will look at it until you are ready) and change the game into *Visions.* Feature questions like, *"Ten years from now, what would you like to be*

160

doing?" "If you could be President of the world, how would you change it?" "If you had all the money in the world, what is the first thing you would buy?" "If you had to relocate to a new country, where would you go and why?" These are not only great questions for warming up the atmosphere, they will also lend themselves to new insights between family members.

If the gathering is going to include several days (Thanksgiving and Christmas frequently call for 2-4 day visits) gather everyone at least once a day for a game. *Pig* is fun and *Indian* is great for encouraging people not to take themselves seriously.

People

Because there are so many diverse ages and personalities at a gathering like this, you'll need to take these things into consideration when you are planning activities. Undoubtedly the most creatively taxing of any party you will give, if you carefully consider your cast of characters, you will be able to find projects that will make even this gathering memorable and fun.

Environment

Decorate with old family photos. I have taken tiny pictures from my little "127 Brownie" camera from my childhood and had them blown into poster size and they turned out great. If you've got old report cards, vintage children's drawings, even old pieces of clothing that people will remember, hang them up. Not only will it be fun to look at, it will stimulate conversation and (hopefully) happy reminisces.

Food

Serve something simple and "Down Home," like fried chicken or pot roast. All the Sundays of my childhood were blessed with great roast beef. Although I don't eat red meat that often today, my folks do, and mashed potatoes, roast, broccoli, and a green salad followed by apple or peach pie (fresh fruit for the non-sugar club) would make a terrific meal that everyone would like. Whatever your favorite family recipe is, by all means feature it.

Time

Gather old family photos, memorabilia, get snapshots copied. Make placecards tailoring the question to the person. Buy a swell puzzle. Rig a table of some kind. Make sure there is adequate of light.

Special Notes for this Party

Some families have a lot of water under the bridge and it is constantly threatening to "boil over." Make sure all the parties have no real *competition* involved and are played for fun. Whatever bad feelings may be lurking under the surface, everyone really *would* like to have a good time (even if no one thinks it's possible). It is possible if there is something fun to do. Make sure you have all your chores done before everyone arrives so you, too, can relax and find a way to have a good time.

5   Regularly Scheduled Parties

Birthdays, National Foot Day parties and Hootenannies really only scratch the surface of possible themes. Those are parties that occur once and then they are over. What about parties that happen within some type of regular framework? This part of the book is dedicated to periodic parties for various purposes.

Event

Vacation groups. After college, my son and his friends scattered to various parts of the East Coast. Since distance keeps them from spending Friday nights together, he and his wife Adele have hit upon an idea that appeals to me. Several times a year the groups meets for mini-vacations. The group has evolved from singles to couples to marrieds and, most recently, to married...with children.

One of Jamie and Adele's favorite events is the Annual Ski Weekend. Adele's parents are in Florida during the winter, so their summer home in the mountains is provided in exchange for help with opening and closing the house each season. On Ski Weekend, everyone brings food, cooks, helps open the house when they arrive and drain pipes when they leave.

A few summers ago, the group chartered a boat for a week. This year, they are going to rent a house on Cape Cod. Your ideas might involve Mexico, Canada, Arizona or some other nearby vacation area. Other ideas that appeal to me include rafting vacations, craft vacations, or fitness weeks at nearby spas.

I'm always envious of their escapades. Whenever I say, *"Gee, I wish I had a group of people like that to go play with,"* Jamie always says, *"Hey, Mom, just make the effort."*

Guests

Your most compatible and adventurous friends.

Environment

Group decision and responsibility.

Time

Plan event, schedule space, provide food; make sure everyone has the right clothes; assign chores, select activities; collect rents, fees.

Special Notes for this Party

These parties appeal to me more than any of the others in this book. The experience of living for a period of time with close friends is so pleasant that the friendship is strengthened in a way that can't happen with a three hour visit. It's a lot of work to coordinate everything, but it's well worth it.

When my kitchen was finally remodeled a few years ago, I decided to celebrate by inaugurating monthly cooking parties. Although my kitchen is no bigger, one of the great things I did was put a sink on *each side* of the room and get a great new stove that has two oven/broilers and 6 burners. Since the kitchen is so "user-friendly" now, and the kids are gone, this was my excuse to regularly have lots of cooks in my kitchen at once.

Event

Group Cook-Off. I gathered seven other interested participants and we started our cooking parties. The rule was that you had to cook something you had never cooked before. Everyone brought all her own ingredients (except staples). There was no real pressure for a dish to be spectacular because there were so many new and different things to taste. Each guest (or couple) alternated responsibility for a particular dish (dessert, main course, vegetable, etc). We made assignments for next time at the end of each meal.

    This was a successful party because there was never any doubt about the shape of the evening. Guests hit the door, headed straight for the kitchen and began peeling, dicing, rolling and baking. There was much to learn from the other chefs and the food was so delicious that you just wanted to stop what you were doing and eat...all the time.

    Most of the cooks were much farther along in their craft than I was, but they were patient. My creations tasted good, but I don't think I ever got a "10" for presentation.

    We cooked. We ate. We cleaned up. At the end of the evening, we felt so gratified on every level. Not only had we usually eaten very delicious food, we all learned something in the process. A very satisfying experience.

Guests

Eight is best.

Environment

Rotate from kitchen to kitchen if you prefer, just make sure there are pots, pans, utensils, space for all. Group decision and responsibility.

Food

Each guest is responsible for a dish.

Time

Coordinate food assignments, select and gather ingredients.

Special Notes about this Party

With all the emphasis on health, cutting out fats and stimulants, it's a perfect time to regularly gather friends in the search for new recipes that are not only healthy but delicious.

Pizza Night Party

I know a group of about 20 happy people that has been meeting every Wednesday night for four years for pizza. The organizing member felt she was not seeing enough of her friends. Although the group got together for Christmas, Easter, Thanksgiving and Fourth of July, she felt people were slipping away.

Event

Extended Family Dinner. That's how a lucky group of people became involved in what is now called Pizza Night. About eight regularly show up for pizza depending on people's schedules. Two couples function as Mama and Papa. They field RSVPs, order pizza and collect money for food and drinks.

The group really functions as family. They play games, celebrate birthdays and produce a legendary annual calendar comprised of pictures from the group. One person is responsible for January, another February, and so on. Each month consists of two pages: one cover page (a collage of pictures of the group, a recipe, graphic, picture to color, whatever) and the regular graph of days for that month. The January person fills in all January birthdays, Pizza Wednesdays, coming events, etc.

On November 1, all artwork is delivered to the organizer who has the material photocopied and bound. Each member receives a Custom Pizza Night Calendar at their Christmas party.

Guests

Core group of eight.

Food

Pizza, sodas, salads, sometimes take-out Chinese. Anything easy that the group agrees on.

Environment

Home base floats or regular host; weekly or monthly.

Time

Divide responsibilities for food, birthday cakes, organizing, and game supplies.

Special Notes for this Party

Either collect in advance for food, or designate "money-jar" for food.

► Stitch 'N' Bitch

My friend, Georgann Alex started the party I've been dreaming about. She lives in another town or I would be a regular participant, it's all the things I want to do.

The party begins in her kitchen. Although the evening is not supposed to be about food, no one is able to resist bringing fabulous provisions.

After the meal, all adjourn to Georgann's studio where each member hauls out her knitting, crocheting, sewing machine, etc. The activities vary. Currently, one member is teaching the rudiments of sketching. For a while, French was spoken exclusively while knitting.

Every six months, they schedule a *"Cry Night."* You come and just cry and moan if you want. It started out as a goof and has ended up being a real release for the members.

You can organize for any number of activities, and depending on the style in which you present it, it becomes a party. You can hire a teacher of French, yoga, calligraphy, whatever. Invite friends, share food and acquire a new skill and a support group while enjoying a party. All it takes is organization and effort.

Event

Handiwork, French lessons, mutual support. Anything anyone wants to learn.

Guests

Core of eight.

Environment

Group decision.

Food

Group responsibility.

Time

Make sure space is comfortable; select and cook your contribution; bring your craft.

Special Notes for this Party

This party is not only fun, but a way to share, learn, grow, and bond.

I have a friend who starts a book club as soon as she moves into a new area.

Event

Readers Anonymous. This is a terrific idea for not only getting acquainted, but also, a "nudge" for you to keep up on your reading. Donna drops notes in her neighbors' doors, says she wants to meet her new neighbors and invites them for dinner. She invites only women, but there's no reason not to make this a coed group. She fixes a buffet dinner for the first meeting, proposes a once-a-month book club and asks who is interested.

If you already know a lot of folks, you might prefer a phone call to find out who wants to be involved. Once the group is gathered, set up the ground rules. Decide if the meeting will always be at the same place and if everyone will bring food or if the meeting place is to float and the current host will provide the food.

The next order of the day is book suggestions. Once a consensus is reached, everyone commits to reading the chosen book before the next meeting. Feature newest best-sellers, classics or a total hodgepodge.

Group members take turns leading the discussion. It doesn't have to be run according to Robert's Rules of Order. Some spirited, spontaneous, yet friendly disagreements add spice to the evening.

Although the focus of the evening is books, the group can become a wonderful support group for one another and the topics of conversation far-reaching.

Guests

Core of eight.

Environment

Group decision.

Food

Group responsibility.

Time

Read book decided upon. Have some ideas to suggest for next meeting.

Special Notes for this Party

Set a specific time during the evening that next month's selection will be decided on.

Jill, a stage manager friend of mine loves to sing. Instead of just fantasizing about how great it would be to get together with a group of people and sing every week, she organized herself and her friends for a great adventure.

Event

"Smith" Family Singers. Jill cajoled a friend, who used to teach choir, into being the music director and enlisted a group of like-minded friends. Now her group's Monday nights are spent singing four-part harmony and Thursdays find Jill studying sight reading. The group rehearses at a church basement and invariably stops at a nearby restaurant on the way home to prolong the experience.

The singers signed on for a finite amount of time and staged a fun recital at the end of the term featuring their hard work as well as delicious food. The group has decided to continue and will not only perform again for their friends, but now have scheduled appearances at hospitals and convalescent homes.

Guests

Core group of eight.

Food

Nearby restaurant.

Environment

Group decision.

Time

Arrange for musical director, plan recital.

Special Notes for this Party

Not everyone may want to get as formal as Jill did and have their own, real live "music director," but you will need someone to act as leader. This post requires preparation and initiative, so choose carefully.

Finding a real goal, such as singing at a benefit a few months hence, or a Christmas party will help focus the group into a committed organism. It is important to have a "definite time commitment." People are very busy and it's easier to assume an obligation if you know there is a beginning and ending date. You can always start another project after a little rest.

A Few Pointers

Have a large party pool. For continued success, you must have more group members than are required for each week's party. People are hesitant to commit to an activity if they feel they cannot make alternate plans without inconveniencing other members of the group.

I know of a play group that meets every Sunday afternoon. They've got a party pool 25 people deep. The first eight to check in on Monday of the party week are those who get to come. This gives everyone an option and also creates a certain elitist appeal: not *everybody* gets to come.

If it's a weekly party, it's better to choose a weeknight instead of asking someone to routinely give up a weekend night. I'm sure that is one of the reasons Pizza Night is such a success.

Also, *spread the responsibility* around. Unless you have help and/or a secretary, it's a drag to be the constant organizer. If you're in a group that someone else has put together, offer to shoulder some of the burden. If you are thinking of putting together a group, attempt to enlist some cohorts. Any task is more enjoyable with help.

One Unifying Moment

All parties need one unifying moment. Whether you call it that, whether anyone realizes what went on, no matter what else goes on. Whether there was square dancing, eating, or foot painting, it's important to have one moment when the event stops and the guests are all involved with one another and make contact on a person-to-person level.

Maybe you'll take a group portrait or have a story written one line at a time by each guest to be read aloud with the group assembled at the end of the party. A group toast to each other from the host to the guests and/or vice versa or just the prize-giving. Whatever the activity is, it's nice to end the party with the group gathered.

We are all one. We are all still children. Our bodies get older, but as Gertrude Stein said: *"We are all the same age on the inside."* Educator, writer, health advocate, author Norman Cousins wrote in <u>Anatomy of an Illness</u> that he cured himself of a dread disease by regularly scheduling a time for laughing and playing.

So, get on with it. Call up your friends. Start playing. Your first party doesn't have to be perfect, and the more you do it, the easier it will be. The one common refrain from people nearing the end of their lives is they wish they had taken more time to be with their families and friends.

Start now. Have a party.

Recipes

6 Recipes

Chinese New Year

Won Ton Nosh

Buy a package of won ton skins. The first time I bought won ton skins, I didn't know whether to ask in the meat market or wherever. To save you that embarrassment, I will tell you that they will be refrigerated or frozen in the chinese food section.

If they are frozen, allow them to defrost. Then cut them into one inch strips and deep fry. It takes a while and makes a lot, so don't wait until the last minute. Drain and then store in big zip lock bags once they are cool. They will keep several days, but are best when fresh. Either serve them with beverages before the meal or put them in a basket and pass them around the table during the meal as the bread.

Vegetable Fried Rice

- 1 sweet red pepper, chopped
- ½ c broccoli
- ½ c snow peas
- ½ c chopped scallions
- 2 T olive oil
- 2 c of cooked white or brown rice

Stir fry each vegetable separately for 3 minutes. When the last vegetable is fried, return the others to the wok or fry pan, add rice and stir together until all vegetables are blended and the rice is hot. Turn into warm serving dish. You can add or subtract any vegetable depending on the season.

Chicken New Year

- 1 ½ pounds chicken breasts, skinned, boned, cubed

- 1 egg white slightly beaten
- salt to taste
- 1 ½ t cornstarch
- 2 c peanut oil
- 1 ½ T Hoising sauce
- ¾ T soy sauce
- 1 bunch asparagus (washed and cut on the diagonal)

Dip chicken in the combined egg white, salt, and cornstarch. Set aside. Heat oil in wok until hot. Stir fry chicken pieces for about 3 minutes. Drain well and set aside. Pour all but 2 T oil from wok. Add scallions and Hoising. Stir well. Add soy sauce, stir just enough to blend, put chicken back in and stir 30 seconds. Serve immediately.

Celery Heart Salad

- 2 Celery hearts (all but the trees of the celery)
- 1 ½ T soy sauce
- 1 T sesame oil
- 1 T vinegar
- 4 Cherry tomatoes

Cut celery hearts into 1" lengths. Shred each piece lengthwise into tiny strips. Quarter the tomatoes and toss with celery. Chill for at least 15 minutes. Combine soy, sesame oil and vinegar and pour over celery strips before serving.

Valentine Making Party

Cupid Ravioli

Basic ravioli recipe. If you have a pasta making machine, use their recipe or whatever you are used to. It's all pretty much the same. Sometimes I put dry herbs (dill, basil, and oregano in with the flour) and sometimes I use one less egg. If you have never made pasta dough before, it sounds complicated, but it's really not.

- 3 ½ c flour
- 5 eggs
- 1 T oil
- 1 t salt
- 1 egg beaten with a little water
- 1 c prepared pumpkin
- 1 t basil
- 1 t oregano
- 1 stick unsalted butter
- 1 bunch of parsley

Make a mound with the flour on a pastry board and make a little well at the center. Beat the eggs in a bowl with oil and salt and pour into the center of the well. Work with your hands and mix the flour into the eggs a little at a time until it is all combined. Then knead it with both hands until it is very firm and smooth. Dip a cloth into water and *really* wring it out well. Wrap the ball of dough in the cloth and allow it to "rest" for 30 minutes.

When the dough is ready, divide it into two balls. Roll each ball of dough into thin sheets. If you are using a heart shaped cookie cutter, measure how many hearts you will get to a row and drop spoonfuls of pumpkin accordingly. When the cookie sheet is full, place the other sheet of dough over it. Brush the top with the beaten water and egg. Press firmly all around the mounds of pumpkin with your fingertips before cutting with cookie cutter. You can also cut heart shapes with a pastry cutter.

Line hearts on a tray and cover with a lightly floured cloth. Cook a few at a time in *plenty* of rapidly boiling water for five minutes and remove with a slotted spoon to a colander. Keep them in covered bowl in a warm oven until ready to serve.

Sauce

- 2 scallions (finely chopped)
- 2 c chicken or vegetable stock
- 1 T fresh sage (minced)
- 1 t fresh thyme (minced)
- 4 T unsalted butter
- 1 c heavy cream

Place stock in a saucepan (on low heat) and add the shallots. Reduce to ½, add cream and reduce again by ½. Then whisk in butter, sage and thyme. Cut the butter into chunks and add slowly. When ready to serve, add ravioli to the sauce and bring to boil. Arrange four or five hearts on a plate and spoon the sauce over them. Garnish with parsley and a Valentine on a toothpick.

Mrs. Cupid's Flan

Flan is a pretty traditional recipe and most recipe books will come through for you. Here is one I like a lot:

- 4 c milk
- 1 ¼ c sugar
- 1 ½ T vanilla
- 4 egg yolks
- 5 whole eggs

Combine milk, sugar, and vanilla in saucepan. Bring to boil, stirring constantly so it does not stick to bottom of pan. Remove from heat and cool. In separate bowl, mix, without beating, yolks and whole eggs. Add 1 c milk mixture and blend well. Return egg mixture to remaining milk mixture in saucepan and mix well. Pour into 6 (4 ½") flan molds. Place in baking pan filled with about 1" water. Cover with foil and bake at 325° for 1 ½ hours or until custard becomes firm. Serve cold with Mr. Cupid's sauce.

Mr. Cupid's Sauce

- 1 pint whipping cream
- 1/2 c fresh or frozen strawberrie
- Add 2 t of sugar to taste, or not

Whip cream until it holds a peak. Puree the strawberries and stir them into the cream to make a pretty pink color.

Dessert Taco

- 1 package large soft flour tortillas
- 1 pint vanilla yogurt (preferably Altadena Naja)
- ½ c Grape nuts or wheat germ, (for crunch)
- Whatever fresh fruits are available, get a range of color, my favorite combination is sliced strawberries, blueberries, kiwi, peach, and plums.

Quarter the tortillas and fry in your favorite oil. Drain. Slice fruit into individual bowls. Put the grapenuts in a bowl, too. *Shortly before serving* assemble the tacos by spreading with a layer of vanilla yogurt, sprinkling a faint layer of grapenuts or wheat germ and then sprinkling an assortment of fruit on each taco...as many colors as possible. Serve on individual serving plates at table or on a lovely platter for buffet.

**Famous Lovers'
Chinese Chicken Salad**

Almost every recipe book has a chinese chicken salad recipe. Here is one of my favorites.

- 1 (6 ¾ ounce) package rice sticks
- oil for deep frying
- 1 head lettuce, chopped
- 3 c diced or shredded cooked chicken

- 6 T toasted sliced almonds
- 1 small can mandarin oranges

Deep-fry rice sticks in hot oil until puffed. Drain. Combine everything in large bowl and toss with Dressing to taste. Makes 6 servings.

Dressing

- 2 c mayonnaise
- 1 ¼ t Worcestershire sauce
- 2 t soy sauce
- 2 t oil
- 1 T plus 1 t prepared mustard
- ⅛ t lemon juice

Combine mayo, Worcestershire, soy, oil, mustard and lemon juice and blend well. Makes about 2 cups

Veggie Lover Mold*

- 1 envelope Knox gelatin
- 1 can tomato soup (condensed)
- ¼ c water
- 8 ounce cream cheese
- ½ c steamed, chopped broccoli
- 1 c mayo
- ½ c diced celery
- ½ c diced onion

Soften gelatin in ½ c warm water and set aside. Heat tomato soup with 1/4 c water and bring to boil. Reduce heat. Beat in cream cheese. When smooth, remove from heat. Cool slightly. Add broccoli, mayo, celery, and onion. Mix well. Blend in softened gelatin.

Pour into well oiled heart-shaped mold.** Chill. Transfer salad from mold to platter. Garnish with radish slices and celery slices or small cucumber slices. * Tastes better if made a day or two in advance.

** Needs to hold 6 c.

Strawberry Pie

- 8 ounce pkg. of softened cream cheese
- ⅓ c (or less) honey
- 2 T orange juice
- 2 T cream

Beat all ingredients with mixer and pour in prepared and baked pie shell.

President's Day Parties

George's Pasta

- 1 pound linguini
- 2 or 3 cloves minced garlic
- enough olive oil to barely cover the bottom of large size skillet
- 2 sweet red peppers or 2 chopped fresh tomatoes or both
- a handful of chopped parsley
- 2 T fresh chopped basil
- a really big pinch of salt

Fill a large pot with water. When it is boiling, add pasta. Cook until al dente (5-8 minutes). Drain immediately. Saute garlic and peppers in the olive oil. Add pasta,* parsley, basil, and salt and stir over a fast flame until all are combined. Sprinkle the tomatoes over the top and stir again. Taste to see if there's enough salt. If not, add some more.

*Add the pasta a little at a time so it will all be well combined.

Caesar's Salad

- 1 head romaine lettuce
- 2 anchovy fillet
- 1 clove garlic
- yolk of one egg
- 1 quarter size dab gray Poupon mustard
- 1 dollop extra virgen olive oil the size of silver dollar pancakes
- juice ½ lemon
- c ½ parmesan cheese
- ½ c garlic & onion crouton
- splash red wine vinegar

This is a very Zen recipe and my favorite Caesar Salad recipe of all time. I don't like anchovies and I *love* this. You can use prepared anchovy paste instead but, believe me, it's not the same. Follow instructions carefully regarding order for best results. You need a large wooden salad bowl with a shallow rounded bottom.

Pulverize garlic, add anchovies to that paste and pulverize, stir egg yolk into paste, add mustard, keep stirring, add juice of ½ lemon, same technique, pour oil into the center of this, stir, generously splash the vinegar. Toss lettuce leaves into this mixture. Add parmesan and croutons, toss, and serve.

Allow guests to salt and pepper on their own. It may not need anything else. I sometimes add a little more mustard because I like the taste to be pretty zingy.

Rhubarb Pie

- 3 egg yolks
- ½ c whipping cream
- 1 c sugar
- 2 T flour
- dash salt
- 2 ½ c diced rhubarb

Crust

- 1 c flour
- 2 T powdered sugar
- dash salt
- ½ c butter

Sift powdered sugar and salt together, cut in butter until mixed and crumbly. Then press into 8-9" pie pan. Bake at 350° for 15-20 minutes. While that's baking, beat yolks lightly in mixing bowl, add cream, sugar, flour, salt, and beat just until blended and thick. Fold in rhubarb and pour into crust. Bake at 325° for 40 to 55 minutes or until set.

Duckling w/Cherries

- 1 4-5 pound ready-to-cook duckling
- salt and pepper
- 4 t cornstarch
- 4 T sugar
- ¼ t each salt, dry mustard, ginger
- 1 16 oz can of red sour pitted cherries (water pack)
- 1 T slivered orange rind
- ½ c orange juice
- ¼ c currant jelly

- ¼ t red food coloring
- 2 T sherry

Cook duck at 350° for 30-35 minutes per pound. During the last 15 minutes of cooking, mix together cornstarch, sugar, salt, mustard, and ginger in a sauce pan. Drain cherries and add that juice to saucepan with orange rind and orange juice. Stir in currant jelly and food coloring over medium heat. Cook, stirring constantly until mixture comes to boil. Boil for ½ minute. Add drained cherries and sherry and heat to serving temperature. Serve with or on roasted duck.

Patriotic Parfait

- 1 pint each strawberry, blueberry, and vanilla yogurt
- 2 bananas
- 1 pint strawberries (if available)*
- 1 pint blueberries (if available)*
- ½ c grapenuts or wheat germ

* Can be prepared with no fruit, just yogurt, but the fruit adds texture and color and is delicious.

Layer each flavored yogurt alternately in champagne glasses (starting with strawberry, then vanilla, then blueberry), with sprinkles of grapenuts, and sliced bananas. End with whole fresh strawberry if available. If it's a birthday, these look great with long tiny thin candles.

Shrove Tuesday

Swell Pancakes

Serve either crepes or pancakes (recipes for both below, use Bisquick, or your own). Topping ideas: Sauteed sliced apple with butter, cinnamon, and yellow raisins; fresh berries of any kind; sour cream; creme cheese; goat cheese.

Basic Crepes

- ¾ c flour
- 1 t sugar
- pinch of salt
- 3 eggs
- 1 T melted unsalted butter
- 1 ½ c milk

Combine first five ingredients in a bowl. Stir until smooth. Then add milk and mix thoroughly. Heat 7-inch crepe pan or non-stick omelette pan and melt 1 T butter over moderate heat. Pour in 2-3 T batter. Cook the crepe until it is golden brown on the bottom. Flip crepe over and brown the other side. Makes about 20 7"crepes

Oscar Party Food

Lee J. Cobb Salad

The Cobb Salad is already a "show biz" concoction having originated at the famous "Brown Derby" restaurant in Hollywood by Robert Cobb in 1936. It's a layered salad where the ingredients are grouped side by side in the bowl. The dressing is served on the side. I've included the basic recipe here. Feel free to do your variation with or without meat or use turkey or ham or both. Tell guests that's how "Lee does it."

- 1 head Romaine, red leaf or butter lettuce
- ½ c shredded chicken
- 1 pound crumbled blue cheese
- 1 pound of bacon (large crisp pieces)
- 4 tomatoes, chopped
- 2 avocados, cubed
- 4 hard cooked eggs, cut into fourths
- 1 cut up scallion

Vinaigrette

- 5 cloves garlic
- 3 T white wine vinegar
- 1 t Dijon
- 3 T walnut oil
- 3 T safflower oil
- ½ t salt
- 1 T fresh chopped thyme leaves

Line the bowl with the greens, put the chicken in the center, arranging other ingredients around the chicken.

Cybill Shepherd Pie

Shepherd's Pie is an English dish consisting of meat, potatoes, carrots, onions, celery and parsnips. Here's one from my mother's old, *old* recipe book. I attached Cybill's name to it.

- 2 T flour
- salt
- 1 t dry mustard
- 1 ½ pound lamb cutlets

- 2 T oil
- 3 onions, sliced
- 3 carrots, sliced
- 2 sticks celery, chopped
- 2 parsnips, chopped
- ½ t dried thyme
- 2 c stock (bouillon)
- 4-6 button onions
- 1 T clear honey

Combine flour, salt, pepper and mustard. Coat cutlets with seasoned flour and shake off excess. Reserve this flour. Heat oil in a flameproof casserole over moderate heat. Add cutlets and fry for 5 minutes on each side until golden brown. Take cutlets out of casserole, add onions, carrots and celery and fry, stirring occasionally for 3 minutes. Add parsnips and fry for another 2 minutes. Return cutlets to casserole dish and sprinkle with thyme and seasoned flour. Add stock, button onions and honey. Bring to a boil, stirring constantly. Cover. Cook at 350° for 90 minutes or until meat is tender.

"What a Turkey!" Salad

The most theatrical dish of all has to be something made with *turkey!* Serve turkey as a main course in the traditional way or put together a creative "Chinese Turkey Salad."

- 2 c shredded turkey
- 2 bunches chopped scallions
- 2 small cans mandarin oranges (reserve the juice)
- 1 head iceberg lettuce - shredded
- 1 pkg Won Ton Skins - sliced and fried (see Won Ton Nosh)
- ¼ c each slivered almonds, sesame seeds (toasted)

Sauce

- 2 T soysauce
- 4 T water
- ½ c each vinegar, ketchup, water

Mix water and soysauce together first, then stir into the vinegar, ketchup and water. Stir all that over a low flame until sauce thickens. Turn off flame, add the reserved mandarin orange juice and let cool. Layer salad ingredients starting with Won Tons, then lettuce, onions, and so on. Put a layer of sauce before you start with the Won Tons again. To keep salad from wilting, put all ingredients in single bowls and combine just before serving.

St. Patrick's Day

Corned Beef and Cabbage

- 1 4-5 pound corn beef brisket
- 2 bay leaves
- 8 peppercorns
- 1 small cinnamon stick
- 12 small new potatoes
- 12 baby carrots
- 12 pearl onions (or 6 small Spanish onions)
- 1 head cabbage, quartered (keep the core in to keep it from falling apart)

Wash brisket and remove bone. In a large pot add brisket, all the spices and enough water to cover. Boil and simmer on moderate to low flame 1 hour per pound or until the center pierces easily. While that is cooking, prepare

The Glaze

- 1 c dark brown sugar
- 1 T dry mustard
- ¼ c molasses
- ⅓ c bourbon

Combine and set aside at least 45 minutes to thicken. When brisket is done, take it out of the pan and use that pan with its liquid. Heat liquid to a rolling simmer, and cook potatoes, carrots, and onions until tender. Then add the cabbage (which cooks very quickly) and cook till that is tender. Serve the brisket on a large platter with the veggies all round, and pour the glaze over all. Serve corn bread with this dish to add to the "Irish."

April Fool's Day

Foolish Quesadillas

Quesadillas are really just Mexico's version of a grilled cheese sandwich. Use a griddle or a frying pan. Take a large flour tortilla, butter one side. Place swiss, Monterrey jack cheese or both, on one half of the tortilla and fold the other half over. (They're easier to flip that way and all the cheese doesn't fall out.) Sometimes I add sliced tomato and/or sauteed onions or chives. Many people use Ortega little green chilies sprinkled in with the cheese. Serve on their own or accompanied by dollops of sour cream and/or guacamole or salsa.

Great Guacamole

- 2 very ripe avocados
- ½ minced onion
- 1 clove garlic
- 1 large tomato or 3-4 plum tomatoes

- good splash lemon juice

Mush all ingredients together. Salt to taste.

Vinaigrette

- 1 T grey poupon mustard
- 4 T red wine vinegar
- ½ t salt
- ½ t freshly ground pepper
- ½ c olive oil

Whisk mustard, vinegar, salt, and pepper until well-combined. Dribble oil into mixture while whisking until ingredients thicken. It will settle, so either do it last or rewhisk before serving.

Strawberry Fool

- 1 ½ lbs. rhubarb cut into 1" pieces
- ¾ c sugar
- ¼ c water
- 1 pint hulled strawberries
- 1 ¼ c whipping cream
- 1 t vanilla
- ½ c powdered sugar
- puree 8 strawberries
- 6-8 whole strawberries

In medium saucepan, combine rhubarb, sugar, and water. Cover. Cook over medium heat 15-20 minutes until tender. Cool to room temperature. Drain off excess liquid, turn into blender, process until smooth. Strain through a sieve into a medium bowl. Refrigerate 2-3 hours or until very cold. In a large bowl, beat cream and vanilla until soft peak stage.

Add powdered sugar and beat until stiff. Puree remaining berries and add to mixture. Spoon into 6-8 stemmed glasses. Top with whole strawberries.

Easter

Cheese Souffle

This is the best cheese souffle I've ever tasted. Interesting and gorgeous and not that hard to do. Guests always go "oooh, ahhh". Do me a favor and don't tell anyone how easy it is?

- 6 eggs
- ½ c grated parmesan cheese
- ½ c grated cheddar cheese
- 5 T butter
- 6 T flour
- salt
- ¼ t cream of tartar
- 1 ¼ c milk

Separate eggs. Butter 1 ½ qt. souffle dish (8" diameter). Dust lightly with Parmesan. Melt 5 T butter. Remove from heat, stir in flour, ½ t salt and mustard until smooth. Gradually stir in milk. Bring to a boil stirring constantly. Lower heat, simmer, stirring 1 minute until thick. Remove from heat. Beat egg yolks, add them to cooked mixture. Add cheeses, beat until well combined. Add tartar to egg whites and beat till stiff peaks form. Fold into yolk mixture (⅓ combine very well, ⅔ just till mixed.) Turn into dish. Refrigerate until cooking (no longer than 4 hours). Preheat oven to 350°. Bake about 1 hour. If you don't refrigerate the mixture, you only need to cook it 40 minutes.

Deviled Eggs

I'm assuming everyone has a deviled egg recipe. Some folks add onions, pimento, garlic, all kinds of things. Me, I'm a purist. I want my eggs to still be eggs. Boil however many eggs you want for 15 minutes. Peel and slice the long way across. Dig out the yolks and put them in a bowl. Combine with miracle whip or mayo until yolks and mayo make a paste (I use about 1 t for each egg). Then spread the egg paste back into the whites. Arrange on a pretty platter with some parsley or other veggies.

Bread Pudding

- 5 eggs
- 2 c evaporated milk
- 1 c regular milk
- 1 c firmly packed brown sugar
- ¼ c granulated sugar
- ½ c melted butter
- 1 T vanilla
- ¼ t cinnamon
- ¼ t nutmeg
- 6 c diced bread
- ¼ c yellow raisins
- 1 ¼ c diced apples

Combine eggs, milks, sugars, butter, vanilla, cinnamon and nutmeg. Blend well. Arrange bread evenly in 15"x 9" glass baking dish and pour egg mixture over. Mix apples and raisins and let stand 15 minutes. Push bread down so liquid covers as much as possible. Cover with foil and place pan in a larger water-filled pan in the oven. Bake 350° 1 hour. Remove foil after first 30 minutes. Make sure the custard is firm. Serve as is or with whipping cream or ice cream.

Kentucky Derby Day

Fresh Mint Tea

Bring a pot of water to a boil. Add 3 sprigs of fresh mint and steep for 5 minutes. Serve hot or as iced tea. Garnish with lemon slices.

Mint Julep

- 1 t powdered sugar
- 2 t water
- shaved ice
- 2 ½ ounces Kentucky (of course) bourbon
- 5-6 sprigs fresh mint

In a silver mug or a Collins glass, dissolve powdered sugar with water. Fill with finely shaved ice. Add bourbon. Stir until glass is heavily frosted, adding more ice if necessary. Do not hold glass in hand (melts the goodies). Decorate with fresh mint so tops are about 2" above rim of the glass. Use short straws so that it's necessary to bury the nose in mint. Mint is for aroma, not taste.

Mother's/Father's Day

Mom's Fried Chicken

Thighs are my favorite part of the chicken and that's all I fry for me. Just thighs and more thighs. When I have company, I fry up breasts, too. White meat is supposed to be the favorite (but, by golly, I see everyone reaching for my thighs - and not under the table, either!!).

- 12 thighs
- 6 breasts (cut into much smaller pieces)

- ½ c each wheat germ and flour
- ½ t salt

Fill a brown paper bag with the dry ingredients. Put a few pieces of chicken at a time in the bag, close it and shake it. Fill a large skillet with an inch of either corn or cannola oil. When it's hot enough to sizzle when you sprinkle flour in it, it's time to put in the chicken. Fill the pan with chicken on a high heat. Only turn the chicken once, so make sure it is brown before you turn it. Cook on high heat 'til brown and then reduce heat and cover 25-30 minutes or until the chicken is done when you cut into it. Drain on paper towel before serving.

Memorial Day/Labor Day

American Grill

If you have a real grill outside to cook these on, great. If not, they'll still taste great if you broil them in your oven. Cut vegetables in half and coat with olive oil, or soak them in a marinade of your favorite vinaigrette or prepared salad dressing for a few hours in advance. Cook cut-side down for ten minutes. Then, turn and cook the other side for five minutes more. Some veggies (onion, green, red and yellow peppers) are small enough to grill as is. Other chunkier veggies like broccoli, carrots, and beets can be blanched first until they are half done and then added to the grill.

A big help with vegetable preparation is a book called Secret Ingredients by Michael Roberts (Bantam Books). It is one of my favorite cookbooks. What drew me to the book (besides the delicious recipes) is that Michael goes into detail about why certain herbs are added. He discusses the whole process of the foods, educating you (and encouraging you) to experiment on your own. With his help, you're always successful.

Flag Day

Patriotic Berries

- 1 c blueberries
- 1 c strawberries
- 1 pint whipping cream
- 1 c sour cream
- 1 c vanilla yogurt

Serve bowls of mixed berries on plates with dollops of sour cream, yogurt and whipped cream so guests can choose any and/or all of the toppings.

Fourth of July

Outdoor Cooking

Wieners, hamburgers, watermelon, American Grill, marshmellows, home-made ice cream.

Vanilla Ice Cream

- 2 c milk
- 1 ½ c sugar
- ½ t salt
- 2 c whipping cream
- 2 T vanilla

Bring milk to simmer, add sugar and salt and continue stirring over low heat until dissolved, add remaining ingredients. Leave mixture to cool. Pour into freezer can. Adjust dasher, cover and place in freezer. Attach motor. Fill freezer w/alternating layers of ice and rock salt. Start the motor.

Halloween

Pumpkin Stew

- 2 pounds yams, peeled, and cut into matchsticks
- 2 large tomatoes, diced
- 1 green pepper diced
- 1 medium sized onion, chopped
- ½ c red wine
- 3 T tomato paste
- 1 ½ t curry powder
- ¾ t cinnamon

Steam veggies for 5 to 8 minutes or until tender. Blend together the wine, paste, and spices. Toss with the vegetables until thoroughly coated. Stew all ingredients until vegetables are tender. Makes 6 servings.

Pumpkin Ravioli

See Cupid's Ravioli

Pasta Zucchini

- 1 medium zucchini (sliced paper thin)
- ½ onion chopped quite small
- ½ c freshly grated parmesan
- enough olive oil to coat bottom of medium-large skillet
- 3 cloves minced garlic
- handful of sliced almonds
- handful of minced parsley
- 1 pound of linguini cooked and drained (al dente)

Saute onions, garlic, and zucchini in the oil. When they are soft, add parsley, linguini, a good pinch (about 1 t) salt and toss all ingredients. Then add the almonds and parmesan and toss again. Serve immediately.

Dia de Los Muertos

Jambalaya

- 2 chopped onions
- 1 c chopped green peppers
- 1 large can tomatoes
- enough wine to cover the bottom of your skillet
- handful of each scallions and parsley
- 5-6 cloves minced garlic
- 2 c water
- 3-5 link spicy Kielbasa sausage cut into small pieces
- 1 pound frozen shrimp

Saute onion and peppers in the wine, but, don't brown. Add tomatoes, cover and simmer about an hour. While that's cooking, brown the sausage and prepare the shrimp either in microwave or by boiling. Consult package for specific cooking time. When the hour is up, add scallions, garlic, parsley and water, simmer another 10 minutes. Five minutes before serving, add the shrimp and sausage and cook for 5 more minutes. Serve over rice. Okra, cornbread, red beans and coleslaw are great side dishes for this meal.

Coleslaw

- 1 medium head of cabbage, shredded
- 1 medium yellow onion
- ½ pint mayo (add more for a wetter salad)
- 3 heaping T pickle relish and a little juice
- salt and pepper

Combine shredded cabbage, onion, mayo, and pickle relish in a bowl and season with salt and lots of pepper. Can serve right away, but best if chilled a couple of hours.

Red Beans

- 2 T olive oil
- 1 T wine vinegar
- 2 cans of red beans
- 2 medium sized onions, chopped
- 2 green peppers, chopped
- 4 cloves garlic, chopped

Saute the veggies in olive oil, then add 2 cans of red beans and cook 20 minutes over low-medium heat.

Political Parties

Creamed Chicken

- ¼ c butter or margarine
- 1 c chopped green onions
- 1 clove crushed garlic
- 4-6 chicken legs
- salt
- coarse ground pepper
- ½ c dry white wine
- dash dried basil
- ½ c sour cream
- 1 T Dijon mustard
- Hot cooked noodles or rice

Melt butter in skillet. Add green onions and garlic and saute until onions are tender but not browned. Remove onions and garlic. Season chicken to taste with salt and pepper. Brown chicken pieces in same butter in which onions were cooked, adding more butter if necessary. When chicken is browned, return onions and garlic to skillet, add wine and basil and simmer until chicken is tender, about 45 minutes. Remove chicken to heated platter. Add sour cream and mustard to skillet and cook, stirring until hot. Do not allow to boil. Pour sauce over chicken and serve with cooked noodles or rice. Makes 4 servings.

Vegetable Pot Pie

- 1 pkg prepared pie crust mix
- ½ c broccoli
- ½ c red pepper
- ½ c scallions
- ½ c carrots
- 2 cloves minced garlic
- 2 T peanut oil
- 2 T chopped parsley
- 1 egg white

Chop all vegetables into bite size pieces (cut the carrots into small slivers) and stir fry in the oil with parsley and garlic for two minutes. Prepare crust according to directions. Roll out 2 crusts, put one on the bottom of baking dish, then place a large portion of vegetables in the middle and sprinkle a T of flour over the mixture. Now add the top crust pinching the crusts together all round. Moisten the edges so they will form a good seal. Be sure to cut an air hole in the middle for steam to escape while baking. Bake until brown - about 25 minutes at 350°.

Baked Apples

- 4 large, firm, tart apples (Pippins are my favorite)
- 2 T honey
- 2 T wheat germ
- 1 T butter melted
- 1 T orange or lemon juice
- ½ c yellow raisins
- ½ t cinnamon
- 1 T chopped pecans

Preheat over to 400°. Scrub and dry apples. Core them carefully without cutting through the bottoms. Peel only the tops, removing about 1 inch of the peel. Put them in a baking dish. Combine all ingredients and spoon into the hollow core. Add 1/4 c boiling water to the baking dish and bake the apples only till they are tender (not more than 30 minutes). Some apples will be tender in 15 minutes, so continue to check. Serve hot or cold with or without sour cream or whipped cream. If you dollop whipped cream over the top, sprinkle a little cinnamon over that.

Thanksgiving

Baked Sweet Potatoes

- 4 large sweet potatoes (one potato for 2 people)
- 1 pint sour cream

Preheat over to 400°. Scrub potatoes and place on cooking rack in your oven. Allow at least an hour depending on the size of the potato. Just before serving, split lengthwise and dollop with sour cream. Arrange on a big platter. Garnish with parsley.

Christmas

Oyster Stew

- 1 pint oysters
- 4 c milk
- 2 T butter
- salt and lots of pepper

Combine all ingredients and put over medium heat. Watch closely. At the instant it begins to think about boiling, remove from heat and pour into mugs. Serve with oyster crackers or saltines.

New Year's Eve

Eggplant/Vegetable

This recipe is adapted from a recipe from La Ve Lee, one of my favorite restaurants, located in the Sherman Oaks area of Los Angeles. I always serve this salad for New Year's Eve for my vegan friends. It is great served with pita or any other kind of bread. Just writing about it makes me want to stop and make some.

- 1 eggplant
- 1 bunch of scallions, chopped
- 1 green pepper
- 4 sprigs of parsley, chopped
- 4 cloves of garlic
- ¼ c wine vinegar
- 1 T lemon juice
- 6 plum tomatoes, diced
- salt & pepper to taste

Slash eggplant all over (to prevent exploding) and bake for a half hour at 350°. Remove from oven. When cool, peel and cut into small pieces. Put everything except liquids into food processor. Process till very small pieces. Add liquids and toss. Serve garnished with radishes, slivered almonds, pickles, sour cream, whatever. It's great.

National Crayola Day

PB and J Sandwich

Make sandwiches the old fashioned way with white bread, peanut butter and grape jelly, or get creative and use raisin bread, banana bread or zucchini bread. Provide strawberry, blueberry, and plum jellies. Make platters with lots of sandwiches. Cut off the crusts and cut the sandwiches into strange shapes. Use cookie cutters or stick to squares and triangles. For real Texas aficionados (like me) bury Fritos in the sandwiches, and for the Elvis fans, use thin banana slices.

"Smith" Family Games

Egg Salad

- 8 hard boiled eggs
- 4 T mayo
- salt and pepper

Grate the eggs, stir in the Miracle Whip, season. Either serve in hot dog or hamburger buns or on pita or flour tortillas. Add fresh sliced tomatoes and sprouts for a great taste.

National Tap Dance Day

Pasta w/Sundried Tomatoes

- 2 T unsalted butter
- 2 T olive oil
- 8 sun-dried tomatoes, finely chopped
- ¼ c fresh basil, chopped
- ¼ c fresh parsley, chopped
- 4 cloves garlic, minced
- 4 red peppers, roasted, peeled, cut julienne
- salt and pepper to taste
- ½ c parmesan cheese

Cook pasta in boiling salted water until al dente. Drain. Meanwhile get all ingredients ready before you begin combining. Melt butter in a saucepan. Add olive oil and heat. Add tomatoes, basil, parsley, garlic and pepper. Saute until heated through. Season to taste with salt and paper. Add to drained pasta and toss to mix well. Top with Parmesan. Makes 6-8 servings.

Square Dance Party

Honey Pear Bake

- 6 pears, peeled, halved and cored
- 2 T honey
- 2 T wheat germ
- 1 T butter, melted
- 1 T orange or lemon juice.
- ½ c yellow raisins
- ½ t cinnamon

- 1 T chopped pecans
- sour cream
- whipped cream

Preheat oven to 400°. Put pears in a baking dish. Combine remaining ingredients and spoon over the pears. Add ¼ c boiling water to the baking dish and bake the pears only till they are tender, not more than 30 minutes. Some pears will be tender in 15 minutes, so continue to check. Serve hot or cold with or without sour cream or whipped cream. If you dollop whipped cream over the top, sprinkle a little cinnamon over that.

National Foot Day

Jackson Pollock Pizza

Here's a pizza different enough to be Jackson's. Instead of crust, the toppings are mounted on eggplant rounds!!

- 2 large eggplants
- 2 beaten eggs
- 1 c grated sharp cheddar cheese
- ¼ c olive oil
- ½ c mushrooms
- 2 T fresh basil
- onion powder
- 1 ½ c wheatgerm
- ¼ c milk
- 1 c grated mozzarella cheese
- 2 small cans tomato paste
- 1 red pepper, roasted and diced
- ½ onion, diced and sauteed
- ½ t oregano

- 1 clove minced garlic

Preheat oven to 375°. Slice eggplant in ¼ inch slices. Mix wheatgerm, thyme, and onion powder together with beaten eggs to make a batter. Dip eggplant in batter and place on greased cookie sheet. Bake 15-20 minutes. Mix spices and tomato paste. Spread tomato mix over eggplant. Top with a dab of onion, red pepper, cheeses and mushrooms. Bake for 5-10 minutes more or until cheese is melted.

Hootenannies

Hoedown Spaghetti

- 6 sweet Italian sausages
- 1 c red wine
- 2 large cans plum tomatoes
- 1 12 ounce can tomato paste
- 1 large onion
- 2-3 grated carrots
- 4-6 cloves minced garlic
- 1 t each olive oil, parsley, basil, oregano, thyme, anise seed
- 2-3 t parsley

Cut the sausages in chunks and brown them. Braise onion, garlic and carrots in olive oil until they're soft. Add remaining ingredients and simmer several hours. Serve over al dente pasta.

Tabloid Party

Enquiring Pasta

Grains and beans are both foods that increase brain function. "Enquiring Minds" will find this helpful in their pursuit of information!

- 2 T extra virgin olive oil
- 3 cloves minced garlic
- 1 pound linguine
- 1 pound green beans
- 1 pound large white mushrooms, cut in strips
- juice of one lemon
- ¼ c white wine vinegar
- 3 T Dijon mustard
- ¼ t black pepper
- ⅛ t each tarragon, basil, salt (mix together)
- ½ c walnuts

Steam beans until until tender (about 6 minutes), add mushrooms. Combine last 6 ingredients and toss with beans. Saute garlic in olive oil in a large skillet. Add cooked pasta and toss. Then beans and toss with the pasta. Throw in the walnuts, toss again, and serve.

Summer Solstice

"Long" Grain Casserole

- 1 c long-grained brown rice
- 2 c water
- ½ t salt
- 1 T olive oil
- ¼ pound sliced mushrooms
- 4 strips diced bacon
- ¾ c chopped onion
- ¼ c chopped green pepper
- ½ c chopped heart of celery
- chopped scallions

Rinse the rice well, drain. Put in heavy saucepan with the water, salt and olive oil. Bring to a boil, then cover with tight-fitting lid and reduce heat to low. Cook for 45 minutes without disturbing it. While that is cooking, prepare other ingredients: Cook bacon until crisp. Pour off all but 2 T drippings. Add mushrooms, onion, green pepper, scallions and celery. Cook until vegetables are wilted. Spoon mixture onto rice and serve with "long" loaves of french bread.

Circus Party

Corny Dogs

Not something I'd like to eat everyday, but hot dogs on a stick are fun and even delicious if you do it right. Here's a basic recipe. Allow 2 wieners per guest. Buy kebab sticks, cut them into 12" pieces and soak them in water for several hours so they won't burn.

- 1 dozen skinless franks
- 1 T sugar
- 1 t baking powder
- ½ t salt
- ⅓ c yellow corn meal
- 1 egg
- ½ c milk
- 1 T shortening
- ½ c flour
- 1 T dry mustard
- cooking oil

Sift together dry ingredients. Cut in shortening. Combine milk and egg, beating slightly. Pour into flour mixture. Stir until smooth. For dipping franks, pour batter in tall glass or spread in small shallow pan. Add skewer sticks, making a handle, or hold onto franks with tongs. Coat franks with batter. Drop battered franks into hot oil, cooking until golden on all sides. Drain, serve hot with mustard.

Happy Birthday Fido/Fluffy

Pizza

Definitely the time to call your favorite Pizza Man. Have them meet you in the park. When you order, ask them to cut the pizza into cocktail size. This is twice as small as usual, it will go farther, and will be a lot easier to handle.

Winter Solstice

Strawberry Shortcake

Buy Sara Lee pound cake or bake refrigerator biscuits. Cut a slice of pound cake, lay it on it's side, spoon frozen (it is Winter, you know) berries over cake, top with a *very* thinly sliced piece of cake, add a dollop of whipped cream or vanilla yogurt and more berries. If you use biscuits, halve them as soon as they come from the oven, and treat the same way.

Pictionary Party

Heaven Coffee-cake

- ½ c brown sugar, packed
- 3 c flour
- 1 c butter or margarine
- ¼ c walnuts
- 1 c semi-sweet pieces
- 1 c creme cheese softened (8 oz)

- 1 ½ c sugar
- 3 eggs
- ¾ t vanilla
- 1½ t baking powder
- ¾ t baking soda
- ¼ t salt
- ¾ c milk

Combine brown sugar and ¼ c butter until mix resembles coarse crumbs. Stir in walnuts and chocolate pieces. Set aside.

Combine cream cheese, granulated sugar, and remaining ¾ c butter, mixing at medium speed until well blended. Beat in eggs and vanilla. Mix together dry ingredients (flour, baking powder, soda, salt), add to creamed mixture alternately with milk, mixing well after each addition.

Spoon batter into greased and floured 10" tube pan with removable bottom. Sprinkle with crumb mixture. Bake at 350° for an hour or until toothpick inserted in center comes out clean.

Trivial Pursuit Party

Trivial Pitas

- 1 package Pita bread
- 1 c freshly grated parmesan
- 5 cloves finely minced garlic
- enough extra virgin olive oil to saute…you'll have to add as you go along

Cut pitas in half, then pull completely apart. Cut again resulting in 8 triangles from each piece of pita. Add garlic to a skillet coated olive oil. When the garlic is soft, add pita and saute. Drain on paper towel. While bread is still hot, sprinkle with parmesan cheese. Transfer to large zippered bag when cool to hold until serving so they won't get soggy. A wonderful treat!

Woodstock Weekend

Black Bean Chili

- 2 c black beans soaked overnight
- 1 bay leaf
- 4 t cumin
- 4 t dried oregano
- 4 t paprika
- ½ t cayenne pepper
- 2-3 T chili powder
- 3 T peanut oil
- 3 medium onions diced into ¼" squares
- 1½ pounds canned tomatoes
- 1 T rice wine vinegar
- 4 T cilantro, chopped

Rinse beans, cover generously with water and soak overnight. Next day, drain beans, add bay leaf, cover with fresh water. Bring to boil, then simmer. Keep adding enough water to keep them covered.

Saute onions in oil in a large skillet until they are soft, then add all spices, cook another 5 minutes, then add tomatoes. The beans are going to take at least an hour. When they are tender, add to skillet, taste and season with vinegar. Serve in a bowl with a dollop of sour cream for garnish and a slice of corn bread on the side.

Life's Other Events

Memory Food

Don't get excited. These foods don't help your memory, they'll just jog it!

- Ritz crackers spread with peanut butter and grape jelly
- Ritz crackers with pimento cheese spread
- Ritz crackers with olive spread
- Vienna sausage with little umbrellas sticking out of them

Landmark Birthdays Over 40

Turkey Wild Rice

Roast a turkey, bake sweet potatoes, split and dollop with sour cream, steam broccoli, slice the cranberry sauce and include this great wild rice:

- 1 c wild rice
- 5 ½ c water
- 1 c yellow raisins
- 4 scallions, thinly sliced
- ¼ c olive oil
- ⅓ c fresh orange juice
- 1 ½ t salt
- freshly ground black pepper to taste

Rinse rice, place in medium-size heavy saucepan. Add water and bring to rolling boil. Once water boils, turn flame down and simmer, uncovered, for 45 minutes. Start checking for doneness after 30 minutes. Drain rice and put in bowl. Add remaining ingredients and toss. Best when it stands at least 2 hours for seasonings to deepen. Serve room temperature.

Divorce/Leaving Home Showers

Chili Rellenos

- 1 pkg. corn tortillas (cut in strips)
- 1 pound of grated jack cheese
- 12 firm, sliced tomatoes
- 1 can whole california green chilies
- 1 dozen eggs (whipped with a little milk & cumin)
- margarine, salt and pepper

In a large well greased baking dish, layer dry ingredients in this manner: tortilla strips, tomatoes, chilies, cheese, then layer again. When you run out of ingredients, pour the egg mixture over the whole thing. If the egg mixture doesn't come all the way up the insides of the baking dish, whip up a few more eggs and add so that it does. Cook at 350° for about an hour. Let stand at least 5 minutes before serving so it can "set up."

Apple Tacos

- 1 package small flour tortillas
- 3 tart apples, peeled and diced
- 4 T butter
- ¼ c yellow raisins
- ¼ t cinnamon
- small container of sour cream

Fry the tortillas in corn oil, drain. Set aside. Saute apples and raisins in butter, stir in cinnamon. Spread a layer of sour cream on each tortilla, spoon on apple mixture.

Games

7   G a m e s

Balderdash

Balderdash is a store-bought board game that involves truth telling vs telling tall tales and being able to figure out which is which. Available at most toy stores.

Charades

Divide the group into two teams. Do it by sex, age, make of car, birthdays in the first or last six months of the year. The host provides enough slips of paper with song, movie, and book titles, as well as real and/or made-up quotations, to give each player to chance to play 5 rounds or so.

Team A sends up Mary who reaches in the game hat (box, bowl, what-have-you) and pulls out a piece of paper. She reads it quickly and has 30 seconds (or however long the groups decides) to begin. She must then get her team to figure out what is written on the piece of paper *without talking*.

Let's say Mary gets the song title, "On Moonlight Bay." When the timer says, "go," she puts both hands to her mouth and then stretches them out toward her audience (the signal for "song"). They now know it is a song. She then holds up three fingers to let them know there are three words in the title.

Next, she holds up one finger so her teammates know that she is doing the first word. Then she holds her thumb and forefinger close together indicating the first word is very small. The team mates say, "In?" "An?" "On?" When they say "On," she points to the person who said it and taps her nose meaning "You're right. On the nose. That's it."

She moves onto the second word by holding up two fingers. Since this word is two syllables, she gets them to say "two," nods yes, touches her nose, but, also holds up those two fingers in a "v" and puts that "v" on her opposite arm on the inside of the elbow. Don't ask me why this means "syllables," it just does. She then holds up one finger (indicating the first syllable) and gives a clue for "moon." She might point to the sky or make a circle or act like she is "mooning" the crowd. When someone says "moon," she points to them and taps her nose again.

They now know it's "On Moon-something" and someone may guess it by now. If not, she has to do "light." She holds up two fingers (second word), holds two fingers up again and again taps her arm with the "v" indicating, "Second word, second syllable." Now she tries to get them to say "light." She could mime carrying something very light or pull her earlobe (which means the word sounds like the clue she is going to do) and then mime "fight." When someone shouts, "light," the team now knows the answer is a song "On Moonlight something." They've probably guessed the title by now, if not, she figures out a clue for "bay" or something that sounds like bay. When her team has guessed the answer, the timer checks the time and the scorekeeper notes it.

Go around several times. There's usually at least one person there who knows how to play who can explain the game. Clue for book title: hold hands open together like a book. For quotation: make quote marks in the air with both hands in front of you. For made-up quotation, draw your hand across your throat (for gag) and then make quote marks in the air. For film title: Hold left hand to eye as though it were an eye-piece and crank an imaginary camera handle with your right hand. Go over all clues with group before hand so everyone will be playing with the same signals.

Clothespin in the Bottle

Since milk bottles are pretty hard to come by, you might use glass jars. Have each player step up to the milk bottle armed with clothespins. Then, reaching out, straight-armed and at shoulder height, attempt to drop clothespins into the bottle. No bending from the waist. Only five clothespins per try. Try to land them in the milk bottles. Designate how many you have to get in the bottle to win a prize.

The Color Game

Go to the craft store and buy a large array of brightly colored tissue paper. As the women arrive, ask them to take two pieces of tissue. One color symbolizing how they feel (emotionally) most of the time, and the second color for how they feel people perceive them. Ask them to tear a hole to put their head through and wear the tissue paper. The "real" feeling underneath and the "cover" feeling on top. While the finishing touches are happening to the meal (and into the meal, if necessary) have each women discuss why she chose those colors. For instance, when I played this at a party, I chose yellow as my "cover" color for I think people see me as very "cheery, sunny, and happy." My friend Georgann, also chose yellow as her cover color, but because she thinks people perceive her as "jarring" which is how she sees yellow. Later in the party, ask everyone to gather and talk about how they perceive each other and choose colors to add to the tissue. They can tear pieces and tape them on or cut shapes out with scissors.

Dictionary

Give everyone a paper and pencil. One person takes the dictionary and chooses a word that he feels most people will not know the meaning of. He announces the word. He spells the word. Each member of the group now has three minutes (or whatever time you determine) to make up a definition for that word and write it down in "dictionary-ese." The person who chooses the word writes the true meaning from the dictionary on his paper.

All papers are folded and put into a hat. The person who chose the word reads off the definitions one at a time while the others vote on what they perceive as the real definition.

Players get five points for guessing the correct definition and one point each for each time someone votes on his incorrect definition as the Real McCoy.

Capture the Flag

The play of the game goes like this: each team has a flag and each team wants to steal the flag of the other team.

Divide into the two teams. Make a circle at each end of the playing area. This marks the spot where the home flag lives and where you want to put your opponent's "captured" flag when you win the game. The hard part is not only stealing his flag, but making sure yours is still there when you bring your booty home. This can be a very rough game if you don't set down some ground rules. It's against the rules to put the flag in your pocket or under your clothes when you are defending or stealing.

When I played this game long ago, we played indoors in the gym. Protectors and thieves were designated (within one's own team, no need to tell the opposition) and the lights were turned out. In the gym, the flag had to be in the free throw circle on either side. You can imagine the mayhem in the dark. If you don't have an all-purpose, pretty empty room, outdoors seems like the best idea. But the dark was surely fun!

Easter Egg Hunt

Give everyone a basket as soon as they arrive. When everyone has gathered, draw for teams and begin hiding eggs. Allow 15 minutes for hiding eggs, 30 minutes for finding eggs. Even if all the eggs are not found, the time limit is the time limit.

Teams turn in their baskets and for eggs for the official count. Prizes are awarded after lunch for all members of the winning team plus for the individual who found the most eggs and for who found the least eggs.

Egg Toss

Each guest selects a partner. Each couple begins tossing a raw egg back and forth while standing quite close to one another. After each toss, they take a step back. The couple who can toss the egg farthest without breaking it wins. A suspenseful and sometimes messy game, but lots of *fun*.

Gobbler Contest

Convert a tall, cone-shaped ("witch") hat into a turkey comb by adding a red ruffle down one side. Pass it around the table. When the hat gets to you, you put in on and "gobble." "Best Gobbler" escapes the dishes.

Indian

Indian is a variation of Poker. The dealer deals one card per person *face down*. The players are not allowed to look at their cards. When everyone has his card, the dealer says *"go"* and everyone takes his card *without looking at it* and places it on his forehead facing out so that everyone else can see his card, but he cannot. Then, each player, after looking at everyone else's card, decides to bet (a penny, a match stick, a poker chip, whatever you decide to play with). The highest card wins.

Many people look around the table, see a couple of face cards, plus people sniggering and decide their card must be very low and they drop out without betting. Sometimes, after the hand is over, they look at their card and find out it would have won, but they have been psyched out by their opponents.

The person to the right of the dealer "opens" by saying *"I'll bet one penny,"* the next person may either decline to bet, bet a penny or decide to raise. Same principles as poker. When the betting is over, everyone looks at his card and the person holding the highest card wins.

Play this game at least once around the table so that everyone has a chance to deal. Even the most stuffy guest has to forego dignity with a card plastered to the center of his forehead. Be sure to take pictures. This is my favorite silly game.

"K's 12 Days of Christmas"

Instead of using the lyrics everyone is familiar with, have each guest make up a word or line. The leader starts singing with *"On the first day of Christmas, my true love sent to me, a ----- in a pear tree."* You might say a Jaguar, a chocolate bar, a day off, or whatever you covet. He then points to the next guest who takes *"The second day of Christmas my true love sent to me - two days off...and a ...JAGUAR (or whatever the first person said) in a pear tree.* The song continues. It's necessary that someone who sings and knows the song keeps it going. If you have less than 12 people, just start over again with the next person in line until the song is over. It may or may not end up being melodic, but it always ends up being fun.

Mother's/Father's Advice

Have everyone make a list of ten important things to remember when bringing up children: *"Be sure to feed them." "Don't forget them at the grocery store." " Be nice to them, you may have to live with them someday."*

Give prizes for Most Unusual Advice, Most Helpful Advice, Funniest Advice, etc.

Name that Mother/Father

This game features questions about famous women who are also mothers. Sample question: *"What famous film star (a mother) was driven to fits by wire coat hangers?"* (Answer: Joan Crawford). Pass out paper and pencils and quiz the guests. Ask about The Queen Mother (Elizabeth), about "The Most Married Mother," Elizabeth Taylor. Include questions about every mother at the party. They can be funny or serious. Give lots of prizes.

Newlywed Game

Feature the engaged couple and choose another couple to work with them. Ask really stupid questions. The format is this: isolate the men in the other room. Ask the "brides" what they think their husbands will answer to a series of questions. *"What's the first thing he thinks of when he wakes up?" "What's the last thing he thinks of before he goes to sleep?"* etc. When you have recorded the answers, the men are invited back into the room and the same questions are answered. The couple with the highest number of matching answers wins. Remember, these people are getting married soon and they're under stress, so don't give them an excuse to fight by asking loaded questions.

Pictionary

Pictionary is a lot like charades, but instead of hand gestures, you draw the clues. You can make up your own game, if you like, but there is an official game that is available at toy stores and it's a lot more fun because there are categories that will give you clues.

Pig

To play Pig you need a deck of cards (no jokers). Deal four cards to everyone. The object of the game is to get four cards all alike. Four 3s, 2s, etc. The first one to get four alike *quietly* puts his finger to the side of his nose (while continuing to play). This continues until everyone notices and puts his finger to his nose. Last person so get his finger in place loses. It's stupid and silly and difficult to keep checking out cards and keeping them going with your finger to your nose, but it's lots of fun. Everytime someone loses a hand, he gets a letter beside his name until "Pig" is spelled out.

Pig Dressing

Pig Dressing is a team relay game involving two Designated Pigs (really good sports). They present themselves on all fours to their relay teams (a team of two) who, at "go" begin to "dress the pig." Over their own clothes, the pigs are dressed in jockey shorts, boxer shorts, and long pants, or some other combination of clothes over clothes. The pig then runs to the other end of the room, undresses himself, then runs back and presents the clothes to the next dressers. This is a game that begs for people with an open-minded sense of humor.

Ring Toss

Have milk bottles, soda bottles, or anything that your "rings" can lasso. Use embroidery hoops or drapery rings. Set them up behind a "line" that participants must stay in back of. Decide how many rings must land on a bottle to win a prize.

Rummy Royal

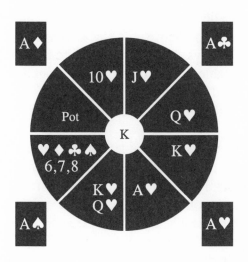

Rummy Royal is a terrific game. The only thing you have to remember about this game is be alert. If you don't pay attention, you won't get to collect your money! No second chances. I love this game. It is a combination of many games and requires a game board that I always make myself. It's sometimes called Michigan Rummy or Tripoli and as such is available in toy stores with their set of rules and a game board. I learned the game 30 years ago in Texas with a made-up game board and have been playing it that way ever since. The optimal number of players is eight. You can play with poker chips, pennies, nickels, or dimes. I'm too nervous to play for more than pennies. Ask each guest to bring 300 pennies to the game. The game board is a circle that is divided into 13 spaces (as per illustration. Use a rectangular piece of poster board about 36" x 24". You can either draw cards on it or do as I do and cannibalize an old deck of cards. As you can see, there are 13 areas that include: 10,J,Q,K,A♥; another A♥; and another KQ♥; one each of the other Aces: ♦,♣,♠; a picture of a "kitty"; another of "the pot." The last space is taken by the "money space" that doesn't come up too often: 6-7-8♥, 6-7-8♦, 6-7-8♣, and 6-7-8-♠. That money is paid when you have (and get to play) the 6-7-8 of the same suit.

225

More about that later. Each player will begin each game by putting a penny (or a poker chip) on each space, so it costs each player 13 pennies to play each game.

Although the game seems complicated when you are learning it, I promise that after a few hands, everything I am about to tell you will become automatic. Just begin following the directions. Don't read all the directions first. Just start going through the motions as you read them. Everyone ante up. That means everone must put one penny on each "money space." Make sure each player puts in her pennies. The dealer will now deal 8 hands with an extra one for herself. This is one more hand than there are players. The hands will not all have the same number of cards. Don't worry. These things work out.

It all starts with "The Auction." The dealer takes the last hand dealt herself and does *not* look at the other hand. All the other players look at their hands and each decides if they like the hand they were dealt or would like to bid on the "extra" hand. The decision is made based on whether or not the hands contain any "money" cards (high ♥ or Aces) or if the best 5 cards (some will have more cards) might comprise a winning poker hand. The dealer is now in control. She can either keep the unseen extra hand herself (if she doesn't like her hand) or she can auction *that hand* sight unseen. If she does keep it, she burns the old hand by putting it face down on "the kitty" in the center of the board. If the new hand is worse than her first hand, too bad, she's stuck. If she does sell the hand, she starts with the person to her left and says, "Would you like to buy this hand?" The bidding starts there and goes around the table with people dropping out and the highest bidder taking the hand. Sometimes the hand goes for one penny and sometimes it goes for 75 cents or more. That money goes to the dealer. Once the hand has been auctioned, it's time for phase two.

The next part of the game is Poker. Now the person to the left of the dealer opens for Poker. You don't have to be a Poker player for this part of the game. I type up four lists if the winning hands and have them strategically placed around the table for inexperienced Poker players. If you don't know Poker, you will catch on pretty quickly. In this particular Poker game, you do not show your cards when you win because, not only do you not want people to know what you have for the other parts of the game, but, people will see what you have as you play those cards down on the table later. You can bluff, but you cannot lie. High pairs frequently win in a game of 8 players because you do not get to draw for extra cards. Poker antes go into the "kitty" so the winner gets not only the proceeds of the Poker but all the pennies already in the kitty from the ante.

The third part of the game is "Collecting Your Aces." Once Poker has been won (and only now) anyone who has an Ace may collect the money on the corresponding Ace in the *corners*. If you have the Ace of ♣, you get that money. Part of the fun is when someone forgets to collect her ace, so don't tell. Just take your money quietly if you have an Ace and hope you get the uncollected Ace next time when there will be twice as much money on it. The "Aces" phase of the game goes very quickly as the person who won at Poker (who collects her Ace and/or gives a brief moment for everyone else to collect. Now starts the play of the game. By taking her lowest black card (Aces are high), places it in front of her and calls out: "Two of ♣" or "7 of ♠" or whatever. There is no choice, you must play your lowest black card. Whoever has the next card in sequence takes it from her hand, calls out "three of ♣" and plays it faceup in front of herself for all to see. This continues until no one has the next card. This happens a lot because one hand has been burned. If you play the "5♠" and no one has the 6♠, you then switch to your lowest *red* card and call it out. When the 10♥ is played, that player takes the money that is on that card, and so on. If you have the Q♥ and K♥, you collect on Q♥, K♥ and on the Q/K♥ space.

Since the Q/K♥ and the 6-7-8 (of the same suit) don't come up very often, the money collects on those spaces and becomes quite sizable by the end of the evening. At some point, whether the "money cards" come up or not, someone will run out of cards and "go out." At that point, she quickly hollers, "I'm out" before anyone collects any other money cards and puts her hand out to collect one penny from each player for every card she has left in her hand. She also gets the money in the pot. If she forgets "the pot" then the next person who goes out gets double money. Once the hand is over, everybody antes up and the game starts once again. At the end of the evening, all money left on the board is grouped together and you play 5 cards dealt face up in front of each player one at a time. The highest hand wins.

A general word: at all phases of the game, if someone forgets to pick up money at the appropriate time, they cannot collect it late. If their hand is in the act of reaching, that's okay, for we know they did not forget. This includes the "pot" that you collect at the end of a round or the Poker winnings (the Pot) or the corner Aces and/or the ♥ money cards. Remember, the A♥ in the center is collected only when that A is played during the play of the game. All money not collected per each hand just builds and the next person gets double or triple, depending on how long it has been since someone won that space.

Sack Race

For the sack race, visit your local produce store and make arrangements to get old potato sacks. Hand out sacks to all participants. Each steps in his own sack, pulls it up as far as possible, lines up on the "starting line" and waits for the signal to go. First one over the finish line wins. This race can be run relay style.

Spoons

To play spoons, you need a deck of cards (no jokers) and enough spoons for all but one guest. Arrange them in a circle in the middle of the table. Deal four cards to everyone. The object of the game is to get four cards all alike. Four 3s, 2s, etc. The first one to get four alike *quietly* takes a spoon and continues to play. As soon as another player notices a spoon is gone, he may *quietly* take a spoon even if he does not have four of a kind.

This continues until everyone notices and takes a spoon. The person without a spoon loses. Keep score by spelling out whatever insult you choose. Each loss gives you one more letter until someone wins/loses by completing the word.

The play of the hand goes like this: after dealing, the dealer takes one or more cards off the top of the deck looking for cards that will match something he has in his hand. Remember, he is looking for four of a kind. If he sees a card he wants, he takes it, puts it in his hand and passes the card he replaced *and* the other cards he looked at, face down, to the player on his right. That player does the same as the dealer, picks up more new cards and checks them out. The cards continue going around the table until someone gets four of a kind. It's important to keep the cards moving quickly, so that people are so intent on checking their cards that they don't readily see someone taking spoons. If you go through all the cards without anyone getting four of a kind, the dealer begins working from the discard pile that has come back to him.

Three Legged Race

Participants divide into couples, stand side by side and tie their inside legs together. At "Go," all entrants race to the finish line.

Wisdom

Each guest is invited to make a list of five wise sayings for the guest of honor. Tell everyone at the beginning of the party they'll be asked to make a list after dinner.

After dinner, gather everyone, give them 3 x 5 cards and pencils to make lists. When the lists are made, either have one person read the advice with an appropriate flair, or have each person read his own advice. Have the advice signed. If you announce categories ahead of time, it will give guests inspiration for focusing their advice.

Buy a photograph album with clear sleeves and put all the advice in the album (provide colored cards for guests to write on that are the appropriate size). The album of advice will be an additional present for the guest of honor.

Wheelbarrow Race

The wheelbarrow race is run with one person as the wheelbarrow and another driving the wheelbarrow. The wheelbarrow puts his hands on the ground, the driver takes that person's legs in his hands and together they run to the finish line.

Who Am I

Who Am I? A game that can be adapted to almost any circumstance. Write the name of a famous person on a piece of paper and pin it on the back of your guest as he walks in. Make sure he does not see his own sign. Each guest will be able to see everyone else's sign. The object of the game is to find out who you are.

You find out by asking questions of the other guests which can be answered "*yes*" or "*no*." After asking two questions of one guest, you must go on to someone else. This way all the guests get to talk to each other and all have something to say. If you ask each guest in the room and still don't know, you just start around again.

It's more fun not to announce what all *names* have in common: it's more fun when the guests figure it out for themselves. There are specific suggestions listed by specific parties throughout the book.

"Callan"dar

8 "Callan"dar

January (Everything's Possible Month)

1	National Save Your Money Day (American Aid to South Vietnam began - 1955)
2	National Science Fiction Day (Isaac Asimov's birthday)
3	Alaska Admission Day - 1959
4	Get out Your Boxer Shorts Day (Floyd Patterson's birthday)
5	National Goof-Off Day
6	Take a Poet to Lunch Day (Carl Sandburg's birthday)
7	National Think About Summer Day
8	Blue Suede Shoes Day (Elvis Presley's birthday) and/or
8	Hold onto Your Head Day (Execution of Mary, Queen of Scots)
9	Don't Get Caught Day (Richard Nixon's birthday)
10	National Good Luck Day
11	Send a Dollar to the Treasury Day (Alexander Hamilton's birthday)
12	National Capricorn Day (Be ambitious, blunt, and loyal)
13	Blame Someone Else Day (celebrated the first Friday the 13th of the year)
14	Take a Missionary to Lunch Day (Albert Schweitzer's birthday)
15	Procrastinator's New Year's
16	There's No Business Like Show Business Day (Ethel Merman's birthday)
17	Invent Something Day (Benjamin Franklin's birthday)
18	Pooh Day (A. A. Milne's birthday)
19	Just Say "Nevermore" Day (Edgar Allan Poe's birthday)
20	Stay Young Forever Day (George Burns' birthday)
21	Aquarius Day (Be unselfish, generous, and idealistic)
22	National Polka Dot Day
23	Practice Your Penmanship Day (John Hancock's birthday)
24	Go for the Gold Day (Anniversary of California Gold Discovery)
25	Eager Christmas Shoppers Begin Today Day

233

26	Popcorn Day (Paul Newman's birthday)
27	Play the Piano Day (Mozart's birthday)
28	Kazoo Day
29	Think Hawaii Day (Tom Selleck's birthday)
30	Let It Be Day (Beatles' Last Public Performance)
31	Eat Brussel Sprouts Day

February (Give Your Heart Away Month)

1	Pessimist's The Year's Half Over Day
2	Wheel of Fortune Day (Vanna White's birthday/Ground Hog Day)
3	A Party is a Party is a Party Day (Gertrude Stein's birthday)
4	National Homemade Soup Day
5	Weatherman's Day
6	Baseball Day (Babe Ruth's birthday)
7	Put Your Gun Away Day (Los Angeles banned sale of semi-automatic weapons)
8	Sweater Day (Lana Turner's birthday)
9	Anchovies Day
10	Send Your Valentines Day
11	Male Centerfold Day (Burt Reynold's birthday)
12	Lightbulb Day (Thomas Edison's birthday)
13	Wash Your Car Day
14	National Smooch Day (Valentine's Day)
15	Jewelry Day (Charles Tiffany's birthday)
16	I Got you Babe Day (Sonny Bono's birthday)
17	Vacuum Your Cat Day
18	Cleavage Day (Helen Gurley Brown's birthday)
19	Pisces Day (Be sympathetic, sensitive, and timid)
20	Clean Out Your Bookcases Day
21	I've Got Your Number Day (first telephone book published - 1876)
22	Invite an Atheist to Lunch Day (Schopenhauer's birthday)
23	Remember the Alamo Day (1836)

24	National Obnoxious Day
25	Go to the Opera Day (Caruso's birthday)
26	Wear Your Jeans Day (Levi Strauss' birthday)
27	National Read Your Warranty Day (Ralph Nader's birthday)
28	National Is It Ever Going to Be Spring? Day
29	National Leap Year Day

March (To Your Own Drummer Month)

1	National Opie Day (Ron Howard's birthday)
2	Green Eggs and Ham Day (Dr. Seuss' birthday)
3	Get a Book from the Library Day
4	National What Did We Do Before Scotch Tape? Day
5	Let's All Chew Bubblegum Day
6	National Mustache Day
7	Burn Your Guitar Day (Jimi Hendrix's birthday)
8	Stretch Your Legs Day (Cyd Charisse's birthday)
9	National Save Your Voice Day (no talking)
10	Get Your Batteries Checked Day
11	Talk Radio Day
12	Talk Mean to Your Spouse Day (Edward Albee's birthday)
13	Everything is Relative Day (Albert Einstein's birthday)
14	Write Your Mother Day
15	National Burp Day
16	Make Everyone Laugh Day
17	Play Possum Day
18	Artificial Intelligence Day
19	Check Your Money Day (first bank robbery in history - 1831)
20	Photograph a Soup Can Day (first large "Pop Art" exhibition held - 1962)
21	Hair Day
22	International Make Ice Cream Day

23	No, I'm the Greatest Day (Howard Cosell's birthday)
24	National Lock Yourself Up Day (Harry Houdini's birthday)
25	Gloria Steinem's birthday
26	National Wig Day (Diana Ross's birthday)
27	Aires Day (Be bold, impulsive, and confident)
28	Eat An Eskimo Pie Day
29	Know Your Stockbroker Day (Michael Milken indicted)
30	Make a Million Dollars Day
31	Don't Buy Grapes Day (Caesar Chavez birthday)

April (A Taxing Month)

1	Do Something Undignified Day
2	Obi Wan Kanobi Day (Alec Guinnes birthday)
3	Go to Sleep Day (Washington Irving and Rip Van Winkle's birthday)
4	Ballroom Dancing Day (Arthur Murray's birthday)
5	It's Going to be a Bumpy Night Day (Bette Davis' birthday)
6	Darn Your Socks Day
7	I've Got the Blues Day (Billie Holiday's birthday)
8	Behave Yourself Day (Jimmy Swaggart Defrocked - 1988)
9	Eat Your Wheaties Day (First seven astronauts selected - 1959)
10	Women's Day (Clare Boothe Luce's birthday)
11	Black is Beautiful Celebration (Jackie Robinson breaks color barrier in baseball - 1947)
12	Stupid Pet Tricks Day (David Letterman's birthday)
13	Dimestore Day (Frank Woolworth's birthday)
14	Brush Your Dog Whether He Needs It or Not Day
15	Get That Stain Out Day (Heloise's birthday)
16	Whew! Day (Income Tax Turned in Yesterday)
17	Take Your Cat to the Dentist Day
18	Psycho Day (James Woods' birthday)
19	Gunslinger Day (Hugh O'Brien/Wyatt Earp birthday)
20	Taurus Day (Be patient, determined, and stubborn)

236

21	Tuna Rights Day (started by the Dolphins!)
22	Be Careful What You Say Day (McCarthy Hearing Began - 1954)
23	We All Grow Up Day (Shirley Temple's birthday)
24	Thee and Thou Day (Shakespeare's birthday)
25	Ambivalence Day
26	Charwoman's Day (Carol Burnett's birthday)
27	Dot Dash Day (Samuel Finley Morse's birthday)
28	International Tie Day
29	Dancers Day (CHORUS LINE finally closed in New York - 1990)
30	Roller Skating Day

"May"be I Will and "May"be I Won't Month

1	National Tall Day (Empire State Building opens - 1931)
2	Take a Baby to Lunch Day (Dr. Spock's birthday)
3	Drive a Tractor Day
4	Long Necks Are Beautiful Day (Audrey Hepburn's birthday)
5	National Bad Guy Day (Al Capone Goes to Jail - 1932)
6	The Martians are Coming Day (Orson Welles' birthday)
7	Play Doctor Day (AMA founded - 1847)
8	No Middle Initial Day (Harry S Truman's birthday)
9	Tear the Tags off the Mattress Day
10	Jigsaw Puzzle Day
11	White Christmas Day (Irving Berlin's birthday)
12	Yogi Berra's birthday
13	Cough Drop Day
14	Star Wars Day (George Lucas' birthday)
15	Get Out Your Nylons Day (First day nylons were sold publicly - 1940)
16	Don't Light My Fire Day (Cigarettes found to be addictive - 1988)
17	National Paint Your Neighbor's Toe Nails Day
18	Blow Your Top Day (Mt. St. Helens Erupts - 1980)

19	Lose Your Head Day (Ann Boelyn beheaded - 1536)
20	Show Your Navel (and everything else) Day (Cher's birthday)
21	Go Fly a Plane Day (Lindbergh reaches Paris - 1927)
22	National Prom Night
23	Rob a Bank Day (Bonnie & Clyde shot to death - 1934)
24	Blowin' In the Wind Day (Bob Dylan's birthday - 1941)
25	Give Your Cat a Bath Day
26	Put Up Your Dukes Day (John Wayne's birthday)
27	National Scarf Day (Isadora Duncan's birthday)
28	National Thank-God-I-Didn't-Have-Quintuplets Day (Dion Quints birthday)
29	Entertain the Troops Day (Bob Hope's birthday)
30	National Bandanna Day (Willie Nelson's birthday)
31	Make My Day Day (Clint Eastwood's birthday)

June (Everybody Gets To Wear White Month)

1	Blondes Don't Necessarily Have More Fun Day (Marilyn Monroe's birthday)
2	Pickle Beets Day
3	National Itch Day
4	National Amnesia Day (What's your name again?)
5	International Violin Day (Stravinsky's birthday)
6	Are You Sure You Want To Get Married? Day
7	What Would We Do Without Ziplock Bags? Day
8	Can We Talk? Day (Joan Rivers' birthday)
9	Let's Get Together and Shave Day (King Camp Gillette's birthday)
10	Mourn for Your Money Day (Withholding Tax Act Signed - 1943 - W-2 Day)
11	Dirty Book Day (The Postmaster General banned Lady Chatterley's Lover from the mail)
12	Gemini Day (Be ambitious, alert, and intelligent)
13	Weed Your Garden Day
14	Folk Singers Day (Burl Ives' birthday)
15	National Irony Day (Indians declared citizens - 1924)
16	International It's About Time Day (First Woman in Space Day - Russia -1963)

17	Bake Your Own Bread Day
18	Count Your $$ Day (Sylvia Porter's birthday)
19	Eat an Oreo Day
20	Take a Bath with a Friend and Save Water Day
21	Get out your 33s Day (first long playing record was introduced - 1948)
22	Longest Day of the Year (Summer Solstice)
23	Annual Mow Your Lawn Whether It Needs It or Not Day
24	National Go Fly a Kite Day
25	Cancer Day (Be moody, sensitive, and impressionable)
26	Good Earth Day (Pearl Buck's birthday)
27	Hum a Tune Day
28	Brother Can You Spare $2.45? Day (Minimum Wage Law Passed - 1928)
29	Wear a Helmet Day (Gary Busey's birthday)
30	Play in the Sprinkler Day

July (Red, White, and Blue Month)

1	Mayberry Day (Andy Griffith's birthday)
2	Hammock Day
3	Teach a Hummingbird to Sing Day
4	National Laugh Day (Neil Simon's birthday)
5	Cookie Day
6	Wash Your Shorts Day
7	"Big" Day (Tom Hanks' birthday)
8	National TV Sports Day (Roone Aldredge's birthday)
9	Lion Tamer Day
10	Hairless Day
11	Animal Cracker Day
12	Eat Your Jello Day (Bill Cosby's birthday)
13	Feel Sorry For Yourself Day
14	International Obscurity Day (Ingmar Bergman's birthday)
15	Excedrin Headache Day

16	Erase Incriminating Tales Day (Accidental revelation of Nixon's secret tape-recording system - 1974)
17	Take Out the Garbage Day
18	Perfect Family Day (Harriet Hilliard Nelson's birthday)
19	Get Out Your Monocle and Cane Day (FDR nominated for 4th term - 1944)
20	Vamp Day (Theda Bara's birthday)
21	Invite an Alien to Live With You Day (Robin Williams' birthday)
22	Try to Get Along With Each Other Day (World War I began - 1917)
23	Leo Day (Be noble, generous, and enthusiastic)
24	Take a Monkey to Lunch Day (Scopes convicted of teaching evolution - 1925)
25	Use a Deodorant For Goodness' Sake Day
26	National 2001 Day (Stanley Kubrick's birthday)
27	All In The Family Day (Norman Lear's birthday)
28	Marry a Millionaire Day (Jackie Onassis' birthday)
29	National Lipstick Day
30	Body Building Day (Arnold Schwarzenegger's birthday)
31	Make a Budget Day (Milton Freidman's birthday)

August (Almost Too Late to Get a Tan Month)

1	International Unmatched Socks Day
2	Touch of Class Day (Myrna Loy's birthday)
3	International Red Telephone Day ("hot line" was installed between US and Russia - 1963)
4	National Backgammon Day
5	Take a Walk on the Moon Day (Neil Armstrong's birthday)
6	Gossip Day (Louella Parson's birthday)
7	Betelgeuse Day (Largest star in the universe)
8	Swim Day (Esther Williams' birthday)
9	Parachute Day
10	Sit in a Tub of Ice Day
11	Lose a Pound Day
12	Get a Tan Day (George Hamilton's birthday)

13	Cowardly Lion Day (Bert Lahr's birthday)
14	It's Okay To Get Old Day (Social Security Act Passed - 1935)
15	Go to the Kitchen and Speak French Day (Julia Childs' birthday)
16	National Material Girls Day (Madonna's birthday)
17	Come Up and See Me Sometime Day (Mae West's birthday)
18	Hunk Day (Robert Redford's birthday)
19	Go to the Track Day (Willie Shoemaker's birthday)
20	National Wear Your Glasses Day
21	Hula Day (Hawaii becomes 50th State - 1959)
22	Conflict Day
23	Singin in the Rain Day (Gene Kelly's birthday)
24	Wear Black to a Baseball Game (Pete Rose was banned from baseball - 1989)
25	007 Day (Sean Connery's birthday)
26	Virgo Day (Be intellectual, methodical, and placid)
27	Show Everyone Your Scar Day (LBJ's birthday)
28	National Bow Tie Day
29	National Plastic Surgery Day (Michael Jackson's birthday)
30	National Burma Shave Day
31	Clip Your Nosehairs Day

September (Let's Get Serious Month)

1	Golden Gloves Boxing Day (Rocky Marciano's birthday)
2	Pierce Your Ears Day
3	Sunburn Day
4	Cook a Great Meal Day (Craig Claiborne's birthday)
5	Back to School Day
6	National Redhead's Day
7	Give Your Grandmother a Paint Set Day (Grandma Moses' birthday)
8	Early Television Day (Sid Caesar's birthday)
9	High Heels Day
10	Spinsters Day

11	Small Town Day
12	Palm Tree Day
13	International Chocolate Day (Milton Hershey's birthday)
14	National Lone Ranger Day (Clayton Moore's birthday)
15	Tune Your Piano Day (Bobby Short's birthday)
16	Wrinkled Raincoat Day (Peter Falk's birthday)
17	National New Nose Day
18	Isolation Day (Greta Garbo's birthday)
19	Wear a Hat Day
20	Everything I Have I Owe to Spaghetti Day (Sophia Loren's birthday)
21	National Rich Villain Day (Larry Hagman's birthday)
22	You Light Up My Life Day (Debbie Boone's birthday)
23	National Wives Day (Mickey Rooney's birthday)
24	Miss Piggy Day (Jim Hensen's birthday)
25	National Ask A Question Day (Barbara Walters' birthday)
26	Libra Day (Be just, orderly, and persuasive)
27	Lie About Your Age Day
28	Sadie Hawkins Day (Al Capp's birthday)
29	National Shrink Day (Bob Newhart's birthday)
30	Chewing Gum Day (William Wrigley, Jr.'s birthday)

October (Turn Your Leaf Over Month)

1	Peanut Day (Jimmy Carter's birthday)
2	Eyebrow Day (Groucho Marx's birthday)
3	Look at the Leaves Day
4	Guys & Dolls Day (Damon Runyon's birthday)
5	Limerick Day
6	Pipe Down Day (first talking movie - Jazz Singer - 1927)
7	Parade Day
8	Take a Fall Day (Chevy Chase's birthday)
9	National Sneakers Day

10	Rats Are Okay Day
11	Kiss Your Car Day (Henry Ford's birthday)
12	Thanks, I'm Not Hungry Day (Dick Gregory's birthday)
13	Hug a Puppet Day (Burr Tillstrom's birthday)
14	national lower case day (e.e. cummings' birthday)
15	Buy a Chrysler Day (Lee Iococca's birthday)
16	It's Safe to Breathe In the Sky Day (Smoking Banned on Airlines - 1989)
17	Sew On Your Buttons Day
18	Eat a Pumpkin Day
19	I'm the Greatest Day (Cassius Clay/Muhammad Ali's birthday)
20	Suspenders Day
21	Garbanzo Bean Day
22	Mouseketeer Day (Annette Funicello's birthday)
23	Stay Up Late Day (Johnny Carson's birthday)
24	Scorpio Day (Be loyal, philosophical, and domineering)
25	"Howdy" Day (Minnie Pearl's birthday)
26	Iceskaters Day
27	Hurry-Up Day
28	Brain Surgeon's Day
29	Don't Sell - Buy! Day (Stock Market Crash - 1929)
30	"Fonz" Day (Henry Winkler's birthday)
31	Last Laugh Day (Jane Pauley's birthday)

November (Turkeys Run for Cover Month)

1	Kiss a Turkey Day
2	National Show Your Teeth Day (Burt Lancaster's birthday)
3	National Housewife Day (Roseanne Barr's birthday)
4	Celebrate Your Honeymoon Day (Art Carney's birthday)
5	Bridge Over Troubled Water Day (Paul Simon's birthday)
6	Follow a Marching Band Day (John Philip Sousa's birthday)
7	Mah Jong Day

8	Lockjaw Day (Katharine Hepburn's birthday)

8   Lockjaw Day (Katharine Hepburn's birthday)

9   Widen Your Horizons Day (borders were opened between East and West Berlin - 1990)

10 Check Your Fuses Day (New York City blackout - 1965)

11 Pay Up Your Credit Card Day

12 Princess Day (Grace Kelley's birthday)

13 Make a Pie Day

14 Plan Your Funeral Party Day

15 Look at Your Flowers Carefully Day (Georgia O'Keefe's birthday)

16 Sincerity Day (Walter Cronkite's birthday)

17 Short Person's Achievement Day (Danny DeVito's birthday)

18 Wind Your Clock Day

19 Clean Your Desk Day

20 Buy a Pig in a Poke Day

21 Wild Bikini Day (Goldie Hawn's birthday)

22 Sagittarius Day (Be practical, imaginative, and mature)

23 Ghoul Day (Boris Karloff's birthday)

24 Stand Up and Give a Speech Day (Dale Carnegie's birthday)

25 Drink Coffee with Your Baseball Day (Joe DeMaggio's birthday)

26 Write a Contract Day

27 Howdy Doody Day (Buffalo Bob's birthday)

28 National I've Got Nothing to Hide/We're Just "Friends" Day (Gary Hart's birthday)

29 Little Females Day (Louisa Mae Alcott's birthday)

30 Dorian Gray's Day (Dick Clark's birthday)

December (Smiling Merchants Month)

1   Nebbish Pride Day (Woody Allen's birthday)

2   Say Hello Day

3   Bake a Biscuit Day (Charles Pillsbury's birthday)

4   National Joggers Day

5   Mickey Mouse Day (Walt Disney's birthday)

6   Put on Your Glasses Day

244

7	Place a Personal Ad Day (Have a date for Christmas!)
8	Pluck a Harp Day
9	National Squeaky Clean Day (Donny Osmond's birthday)
10	National Sarong Day (Dorothy Lamour's birthday)
11	National Knitters Day
12	Blue Eyes Day (Frank Sinatra's birthday)
13	National Weave a Basket Day
14	Christmas Shopping is Driving Me Crazy Day
15	Calm Down, Everything's Going to Be Alright Day
16	Take a Tribe to Lunch Day (Margaret Mead's birthday)
17	Bow Making Day
18	Close Encounters Day (Stephen Speilberg's birthday)
19	Upgrade Your Computer Day
20	Dry T-Shirt Day
21	Exercise Day (Jane Fonda's birthday)
22	Miss Americas Can Do No Wrong Day (Day Bess Myerson was acquitted)
23	Think Your Way to Health Day (Norman Cousin's birthday)
24	National Cozy Night
25	Play It Again Sam, Day (Humphrey Bogart's birthday)
26	International Cold Feet Day
27	International Lose 5 Pounds Today Day
28	Let's Piece Things Together (National Quilter's Day)
29	Floss Your Teeth Day
30	Thank You Letter Writing Day
31	International Kiss Somebody Night